KT-873-282

Reporting the news from

CHINA

edited by
Robin Porter

ROYAL INSTITUTE OF INTERNATIONAL AFFAIRS

LIVERPOOL JOHN MOORES UNIVERSITY
LEARNING SERVICES

Published by the Royal Institute of International Affairs
Chatham House, 10 St James's Square, London SW1Y 4LE

© Royal Institute of International Affairs, 1992
First published May 1992
Second edition November 1992

All rights reserved. No part of this publication may be reproduced, stored
in a retrieval system, or transmitted by any other means without the prior
written permission of the copyright holder. Please direct all inquiries to the
publishers.

British Library Cataloguing in Publication Data

A CIP catalogue record for this book is available from the British Library

ISBN 0 905031 55 5

Text designed and set by Hannah Doe
Cover design by Youngs Design in Production
Printed and bound in Great Britain by Antony Rowe Ltd

Books are to be returned on or before
the last date below.

Reporting the news from
CHINA

LIVERPOOL JOHN MOORES UNIVERSITY
Aldham Robarts L.R.C.
TEL. 0151 231 3701/3634

LIVERPOOL JMU LIBRARY

3 1111 01103 4624

The Royal Institute of International Affairs is an
independent body which promotes the rigorous study of
international questions and does not express opinions of its
own. The opinions expressed in this publication are the
responsibility of the authors.

Contents

CONTENTS

Contributors

Jasper Becker was correspondent of the *Guardian* in China from 1985 to 1989.

Mark Brayne is Diplomatic Correspondent for the BBC World Service. From 1984 to 1987, he was posted in Beijing, and in 1989 he returned to report for the BBC on events leading up to the Tiananmen incident.

Jean Conley works for the *Washington Post*, and Stephen Tripoli for National Public Radio, Washington. Both journalists were sub-editors at *China Daily* in Beijing from mid-1986 to mid-1987.

John David, formerly of the Thomson Foundation, is now a Consultant to the Central Office of Information. He went to China in the mid-1980s to advise on the setting up of Xinhua's International Journalism Training Centre.

John Gittings is a sinologist and foreign leader-writer at the *Guardian* in London. A frequent visitor to China, he returned to Beijing just prior to the outbreak of conflict there in June 1989.

Kelly Haggart is a Canadian journalist who worked as a sub-editor at Xinhua News Agency in Beijing between 1983 and 1985.

Simon Long represented the BBC in China in 1990 and 1991. He is a journalist with the BBC World Service and has contributed numerous articles to the *Guardian*.

CONTRIBUTORS

Robin Porter is a sinologist who teaches at Keele University. In 1979/ 80 he worked for a year in Beijing as a sub-editor in the Duiwaibu, the External Department of Xinhua News Agency.

Roger Smith is London bureau chief of the CTV (Canadian) Television Network. He was posted in Beijing from 1985 to 1987, and returned in 1989 to cover the events in Tiananmen Square and their aftermath.

Elizabeth Wright is head of the Chinese Section of the BBC World Service.

Preface

Foreigners have always had difficulty perceiving the reality of China. Since the first 'opening up' of China to the West in the 1840s, and even before, images of China held by outsiders have been too idealistic or too negative, too much coloured by tales of mystery and exoticism. The continuation of civil strife in China through much of the first half of the twentieth century did nothing to diminish this problem. Since the founding of the People's Republic in 1949, although the developed world has experienced an explosion in media coverage of the human condition in almost all locations, China has been, until quite recently, if anything even less accessible than before.

For most people, understanding of China in the contemporary world comes from news reports about the country and its people. These reports are in turn formed by journalists, both Chinese and foreign, and the Chinese and foreign news media for whom they work. Inevitably, the impression given of a country so vast and complex must be constrained by a wide variety of factors: difficulties with sources, a lack of opportunity for firsthand reporting, personal and editorial prejudices, and overt political interference. Yet, for better or for worse, the process of reporting the news from China not only directly determines how we see China, but also to a considerable degree moulds the policies of our governments towards the world's most populous nation.

Just over a decade ago, China implemented a new policy of opening up to the outside world. This decision had a dramatic impact on the world's interest in China, and also affected the reporting of China. The

Chinese government became more concerned about how China was seen abroad. Chinese journalists, for years labouring under a strict orthodoxy, began to be influenced by the approach of Western journalists brought in to Xinhua and *China Daily* as advisers; they began to take chances. Many more Western media representatives were allowed into China, often with a command of Chinese language and an understanding of the nuances of Chinese politics, which enabled them to report far more thoroughly than ever before on every aspect of Chinese life. This media attention may even, as is sometimes claimed, have encouraged the strong and growing desire for a greater measure of democracy in China, which led inexorably to the tragic events of June 1989.

For these reasons it seemed appropriate in the wake of Tiananmen to examine just how news about China is gathered, edited and conveyed to the outside world, and to look at the constraints on the journalists whose work it is to carry out this task. Accordingly a series of seminars was convened by the Royal Institute of International Affairs at Chatham House in London, between May and December of 1990, with the title 'Reporting the news from China'. Participants included Western journalists who have worked for China's external media, those who have represented the Western media in China, and academic specialists in international relations and Chinese affairs. These seminars provided the inspiration for the present volume.

This book is a collection of distinct essays, each of which is based on the practical experience of its author, and contributes a set of insights into some aspect of the process of reporting the news from China. There are no common assumptions, other than that of the primacy of politics in China, which all who have worked there in the sensitive area of news reporting will readily admit. How to cope with this was a daily concern. Also, a degree of overlap has been permitted in the description of the Chinese news process as each contributor seeks to place in context their observations on this process.

The first part of the book deals with China's own external news media, the press organs that convey the official view of China to the outside world. Chapter 1, which is on the Duiwaibu – the External Department of the official Chinese news agency, Xinhua – looks at the political and non-political factors affecting the nature of its news coverage of China in 1979, before changes began to take place. John David, who on behalf of the Thomson Foundation was instrumental in establishing training facilities for journalists at both Xinhua and *China Daily*, discusses in Chapter 2 the problems encountered in the early phase of the transition. Jean Conley and Stephen Tripoli worked at *China Daily* in 1986/7; in Chapter 3 they assess the degree of effective control that the party exercised over *China Daily* through two crises, that of 1986/7, and that of 1989. Kelly Haggart, who spent two years at Xinhua between 1983 and 1985, gives an account in Chapter 4, based on extensive interviews with Chinese journalists known to her, of the impact on all leading Beijing press organs, domestic and external, of the events surrounding Tiananmen, and of news culture generally in China.

In the second part of the book, journalists who have reported on China for the Western news media make their contribution. Mark Brayne, formerly BBC World Service correspondent in China, comments in Chapter 5 on the sense of distance that is felt by Western journalists stationed there, especially from sources, material and Chinese culture. Jasper Becker, who represented the *Guardian* for four years in Beijing, writes about bias in the reporting of China in Chapter 6. John Gittings was present for the *Guardian* at the time of Tiananmen; in Chapter 7 he describes the difficulties he and others faced in assessing objectively the rapid unfolding of events. Roger Smith reported on Tiananmen for the Canadian television network CTV, and in Chapter 8 reflects on the successes and failures of television coverage. In Chapter 9, Simon Long, who represented the BBC in China in 1990 and 1991, brings the story up to date with his account of the conditions facing foreign correspondents in the post-Tiananmen era.

The book concludes with a Postscript by Elizabeth Wright, head of the Chinese Section of the BBC World Service, on reporting the news to China. Two appendices incorporate further material on China's external news media: Appendix One describes a day in the life of a Chinese newsroom; Appendix Two offers a breakdown of a typical month's output from the External Service of Xinhua News Agency.

It is hoped that in making available to a wider audience the experience and perceptions of some of those who, in one way or another, have taken part in reporting the news from China, this volume will help to stimulate further interest in how our images of China are formed. As journalists and scholars, we believe that the closer we can come to the reality of China the better it must be.

March 1992   Robin Porter

Part One

CHINA'S EXTERNAL NEWS MEDIA

1

Shaping China's news: Xinhua's Duiwaibu on the threshold of change

ROBIN PORTER

Xinhua News Agency remains something of an enigma to Western students of Chinese affairs. Although it was much influenced in style and technique by Tass (the Soviet news agency) in the 1950s, its roots can none the less be traced to the propaganda arrangements of the Chinese Communist Party at Yenan in the late 1930s. At that time, the precarious political position, combined with the memory of the sufferings of the Long March and pride in the achievements of the revolutionary base area, encouraged in the party a desire both to heighten political consciousness at home and to bring news of its success to a wider world. Edgar Snow caught something of the spirit of that time. The conflict between the reporting of news and the more manipulative function of propaganda, apparent in reports of the Yenan era, has persisted ever since in the work of Xinhua, not least in its external news service, the Duiwaibu.

The purpose of this chapter is to examine the way in which the news was shaped for foreign consumption by the Duiwaibu in 1979. Essential to any such consideration must be the role of politics and the party in determining editorial content. There are, however, other, non-political dimensions, including the skills and attitudes of journalists, and various structural factors, which affect what the journalist may write about and how well he or she may do it. These too will be explored. The chapter will begin, however, by setting the scene: looking at the Duiwaibu's role within Xinhua and in the Chinese external news process.

A note must be added on the timeframe of this study. In 1979, the

1

Duiwaibu had only just begun to feel the winds of change that were starting to blow across all areas of Chinese life. At that time its position as the originator of almost all official news from China was still unchallenged by *China Daily*, which had not yet commenced publication, and observations on the way in which it went about its editorial work in particular held true also for most other official news sources, such as *Beijing Review* and Radio Beijing. Also, I was privileged to spend that year at the Duiwaibu sub-editing the news, and was therefore able to observe the editorial process at close hand.

For these reasons, 1979 will be the point of reference for this chapter. In the decade that followed, the Duiwaibu's importance diminished with the arrival of the English language *China Daily*, and important changes began to occur which rendered the editorial and newswriting process materially different from what had gone before, at least up until June 1989. I would contend, therefore, that the conditions described in this chapter have a broader significance, in that they show China's external news work as it was just before foreign influence had begun to make itself felt.

Xinhua and its Duiwaibu in 1979

It is the task of Xinhua News Agency to gather and disseminate news both internally and externally, and to promote the policy objectives of the Chinese Communist Party. The agency is responsible to the party's Propaganda Department, which in turn is under the direct control of the Central Committee of the party. Within Xinhua, a principal administrative distinction is made between the National and the International Divisions. The International Division is responsible for gathering news from overseas, for which purpose it maintains a network of foreign correspondents and Xinhua branches in the major capitals of the world. This material is edited at Head Office in Beijing, and is made available to other press organs in China, which take from it selectively. The International Division also publishes in the *Xinhua Bulletin* a daily digest of news from overseas, incorporating material from its own correspondents and from other news agencies.

The National Division of Xinhua is made up of both Domestic and

External Departments. The Domestic Department gathers and disseminates news within China through a network of branches in the principal cities and towns, providing a major source of information for provincial newspapers. The External Department, the Duiwaibu, is responsible for disseminating abroad news about developments in China. It did this in 1979 by maintaining wire-service links with foreign correspondents in Beijing and with the bureaux of foreign news agencies in Hong Kong and Tokyo. Then, as now, it published in full its wire-service reports in the *Xinhua Bulletin* on the day after their transmission – the so-called 'red news'. In addition, the Duiwaibu provides some finished material on developments in China to other external organs of the Chinese press, such as Radio Beijing, *Beijing Review* and *China Reconstructs*.

Other important units within the Xinhua organization are: the Features Section, concerned with the preparation of feature-length articles about China, which are offered for sale to magazines and periodicals abroad; the Photographic Section, a vast semi-autonomous bureaucracy charged with the task of producing and disseminating illustrative material to support the written output of Xinhua and other press organs, and a small, but efficient, Research Section, whose task is to monitor the quality of news output and to find ways of improving it.

Within the Duiwaibu, routine work is handled by the staff of its political, economic and cultural sections, and by journalists who are chosen for either the morning or the evening work-team on any given day. Broadly speaking, the work-team deals with events of pressing importance as they come up, such as major policy speeches, visits of heads of state, or the proceedings of the party or of People's Congress, whereas the staff of the regular sections prepare stories following a plan of work that is set by frequent meetings of the senior cadres within each section. Each section puts out stories about events in China within its sphere that are considered likely to be of interest to outsiders, or that are of political significance in the view of the party.

In 1979, much of the work was done in the first instance in Chinese and then translated into English, although an increasing effort was being made to encourage journalists to write their material in English from the start. The English-language output of the Duiwaibu is always the largest,

3

and constitutes the basis from which a smaller number of items are translated into French, Spanish and Arabic. Japanese and Russian-language translations are prepared directly from the Chinese. The information on which stories are based comes to the Duiwaibu in a number of ways. Some stories originate with the Xinhua branches in China's major cities and towns, and are in the form of a text sent in by post, on the wire or, in really urgent cases, by telephone. The text may then be modified by journalists at Head Office. Other stories are taken from national or local newspaper reports by journalists at Head Office whose task it is to scan these papers. Still others are taken from specialist journals or from publicity handouts by organizations such as Luxingshe, the China Travel Service. Sometimes a government ministry will issue a memorandum intended as the basis for an external Xinhua release, or will telephone Xinhua with a statement. This happens most frequently with the Defence Ministry and the Foreign Ministry. Finally, a growing number of stories in 1979 were being researched through first-hand investigation by journalists of the Duiwaibu, or by staff of the Domestic Department of Xinhua, although generally the stories were centred on or around Beijing.

The passage of a story from first writing to release by the Duiwaibu is relatively straightforward. A journalist working within one of the Duiwaibu's sections will write up his story in English using his own or other material. It may or may not be inspected by the section head, and will then go to a foreign native-speaker for proof-reading and comment. It then passes to the editor for that day, who will give it careful scrutiny. He may approve it without alteration, send it back for revision, or in a very few cases decide to withdraw it altogether. Once passed by the editor, the story would normally receive a quick inspection from the head of the Duiwaibu or other senior journalist, and then be sent up for immediate transmission by wire and subsequent publication in the *Xinhua Bulletin.*

Shaping the news
The party's leading role

Undoubtedly the most important conceptual dilemma facing the journalists of the Duiwaibu in their work is the dichotomy that clearly exists between the reporting of news and the dissemination of propaganda. This dilemma is a consequence of the leading role assumed by the communist party in news work in any Marxist state.

There are those who would seek to argue that the entire output of the Chinese news media, whether domestic or external, may be considered to be propaganda, in that all news releases are intended to promote the broad objectives of the party. In my view, however, an assertion of this kind offers only superficial truth, and does not take into account the complexity of the tension between the news and propaganda functions of Xinhua and among other branches of the media. This tension, which can be seen in the Chinese media as a whole, is implicitly recognized in the document *Newswriting* (Xinwen Xiezuo, Yunnan University, tr. Jennifer Grant, Australian National University, 1979), which was distributed to young journalists in the early 1970s to guide them in their work. This document, which still has relevance today, asserts that:

> news work is an important medium of communication between the party and the masses, an important means of propagating the general and specific policies of the party, of making the masses understand quickly, [and] of turning [the policies] into material strength. Thus, the good management of the proletarian news media is an extremely important fighting task of the party.

It goes on to say that journalists

> must acquire a style of work of penetrating deeply into the realities of life, carrying out investigation and research. News is the reflection of real life. To write good manuscripts, one must penetrate the front line of the three great revolutionary movements, go amongst the masses, find the subject matter, study the problems, and unearth the many aspects of the abundant and profound substance of life.

5

Thus the journalist is faced with the dilemma that he must both report accurately on all aspects of life and single-mindedly propagate the policies and perceptions of the party. Where the party, or party officials, are unwilling to recognize the true facts of a situation, conflict is bound to arise. How then does the party keep control at the Duiwaibu?

The director of Xinhua is responsible to the Propaganda Department of the party, and through that department to the party Central Committee. More than most units, Xinhua is an extension of the party. Control is exercised in part through the hierarchical system, according to which all individuals in positions of trust and responsibility are party members, sworn to uphold the decisions and objectives of the party. The greater the responsibility, the more committed and experienced will be the party member occupying the position. Because Xinhua is a particularly sensitive work unit, a transmission belt for party policy, very great care is taken over matters of promotion, and over who should occupy positions of authority.

It is a duty of all party members to be well-informed at all times about matters of party policy. The Propaganda Department has the task of monitoring closely the decisions of the Central Committee, and of making sure that these decisions are publicized and widely understood. Xinhua takes its cue from the Propaganda Department, making sure that directives and matters of current concern are reflected in news work. The Duiwaibu in turn must determine what news is appropriate to disseminate internationally; in 1979, its clear-cut duty was to present as favourable and credible a view of China abroad as possible.

The senior staff of Xinhua, and of the Duiwaibu, would therefore meet regularly to discuss the work of the Central Committee, and in particular to lay down guidelines for more junior staff as to what should be covered in news reporting and how in general terms it should be presented. On the external side, the head of the Duiwaibu would then confer at regular intervals with his most senior staff, including the section heads, to convey these concerns to them and to discuss how best they might be translated into news items for external release. Each section head would then draw up a rough plan of work for anything from a few days to a month ahead, ordering priorities and assigning staff to particular stories. Small groups and individual journalists carried out the work. In this way the Duiwaibu functioned to reflect the party's will in international news work.

This process was reinforced by regular meetings for political study which all journalists were obliged to attend. The meetings had the dual purpose of ensuring that Xinhua staff understood the party's current concerns and were orthodox in their thinking about them, and of providing further background information to the stories in the news, thus 'helping' journalists with their work.

Final reinforcement of the party line occurred with the editorial checks on the work of Duiwaibu staff. As noted above, news would normally either be taken from an existing official newspaper or be written from scratch with guidance from senior journalists within the Duiwaibu. It would then be checked and re-checked by the section head, by the editor for the day, and sometimes by the head of the Duiwaibu before it would be allowed out on the wire. Occasional errors of syntax of English translation would get through this process, but errors of line almost never did; the Duiwaibu carried the responsibility for ensuring that China's policies were understood overseas, and political errors were unacceptable. In this way, the propaganda function of the Duiwaibu remained paramount, although this did not exclude a secondary role in the dissemination of genuine news.

The political dimension expressed in style and content

The primacy of politics in Xinhua's approach to news work led to certain practices that set the Duiwaibu's coverage of developments in China apart from that of Western journalists, or indeed from journalism itself in the West. It is appropriate to examine some of these briefly in order to try to identify more precisely the influence of the party line on the external news. The discussion that follows is based wholly on an analysis of the Duiwaibu's output in 1979, although the specific references have been omitted.

To begin with, in 1979 the Duiwaibu reported almost exclusively good news, to the extent that many outsiders would consider a significant proportion of its material not to be news at all. There was a tendency also to be didactic and to deliver homilies, even in news coverage intended for external release. Domestic writing-style was frequently carried over to news stories written for overseas. The conflicting views of powerful individuals within the party were often represented side by side and without explanation, safer for the journalist but confusing for the reader. If public opinion was represented in an article, usually only the views of citizens supporting the party line were cited. Sometimes trial balloons were floated in the external news for political reasons.

Complex and perhaps controversial material was often rendered in a simplistic way, and the general preference was for a pedestrian observation over one that might have some insight. On some occasions the facts of the matter at hand were quite plainly misrepresented. Political considerations were responsible for important lacunae in the coverage of events, and fundamental shifts in policy over the years meant that what was painted white at one stage must be represented as black at another. This was true as much for individuals as for the many strands of policy on which the official view changed dramatically at various times before, during and after the Cultural Revolution. Thus a foreign colleague of mine had the surreal experience of 'polishing' a story propounding Vice-Premier Deng Xiaoping's line on some matter, written on recycled paper on the back of which was printed a story in French from the early 1970s strenuously condemning Deng and everything he stood for.

Theoretical articles based on contributions by senior party officials to *People's Daily* or *Red Flag* were reproduced verbatim and usually without comment, leaving the foreign journalist to interpret terms like 'social imperialism' and 'hegemonism' or to work out for readers overseas the implications of the doctrine of historical materialism. Terminology used to describe people was often a guide to changing political fortunes. When large groups of people gathered together, as for example delegates to a congress, they were always represented as speaking with one voice, whether this was so or not.

There was finally a tendency to drop items for political reasons when they were clearly still news, or to omit mention of developments of which the world was already aware because they were considered to be, for reasons quite unfathomable to the outsider, damaging to China.

All these practices had their roots in the political imperatives of

Xinhua's role in Chinese society. That they were carried over to its news coverage for overseas is itself of interest, since truly effective propaganda directed outside China would have been much more subtle. There was a strong sense in the Duiwaibu in 1979 that its news stories were like Werner von Braun's rockets; where they came down was not their department. The reasons for this may have been as much cultural as political, and this dimension to the news will be explored later.

Skills and attitudes

If the shape of the news from China in 1979 was much influenced by political considerations, it was also quite materially affected by other factors that were not at all political in any direct sense. Foremost among these were the skills and attitudes of the Duiwaibu's journalists.

Although some staff were quick to recognize a story, others were unable to distinguish between what was newsworthy and what was not. In consequence, stories not infrequently appeared that were so vague and lacking in precise information as to be not worth releasing. Or an item might contain information of a descriptive kind, but would have nothing about it that would make it news. Even within the limitations imposed by the need to follow closely the policy concerns of the party, opportunities existed for a more thoroughgoing exploration of the issues. Journalists were not generally sufficiently well-educated or well-motivated to sit down and consider carefully what sort of information should be in a story to make it logical and complete, or indeed what sort of developments deserved coverage.

In many cases, journalists lacked the skill actually to go out and report on developments, preferring to rely on other press organs, such as *People's Daily,* to provide both the facts themselves and the interpretation of events. There was reluctance too to seek personal interviews with Chinese leaders to clarify their views, although the same reticence was not always present when visiting foreign dignitaries were involved. By the same token, Chinese leaders frequently chose to publish their major speeches or 'guest commentaries' in the domestic Chinese press first, leaving the Duiwaibu to pick them up later. For example, when Deng Xiaoping wanted to address an international audience while visiting

Japan in 1979, he gave his interview not to Xinhua but to the Japanese News Agency instead.

The level of skill was reflected too in the style and terminology used in some Duiwaibu releases. Recurring expressions were the result of a too-literal translation of idiomatic Chinese, such as the ubiquitous term 'backbone' being used as a noun to denote a person of great moral strength. Other terms represented usage that was no longer current in most of the English-speaking world, and that reflected the literature used in the teaching of English in China during the years of isolation. Still other habitually used phrases conveyed only the vaguest idea of what was meant, for example 'tapping potential', 'appropriate authorities' and 'department concerned'. There were finally those oddities that had for no apparent reason achieved a permanent place in the Duiwaibu's vocabulary. Thus the 'personage' had a 'heart-warming conversation' before 'leaving for home' to 'popularize new techniques'.

Many Duiwaibu stories had an economic theme, consistent with the emphasis that was beginning to be placed by the party on development and modernization. Within the Economic Section of the Duiwaibu, few staff had any specific knowledge of economics, although some had learned on the job and acquired a degree of expertise. Still apparent was the Marxist tendency to feel that quantification means precision, even in instances in which a percentage or an absolute number seemed highly implausible or wholly inappropriate to the subject at hand. More Chinese was the practice of rounding out numbers, what might be termed the '100 schools 10,000 li' approach, a habit that seemed odd to outsiders. All too frequently inaccuracies crept in, especially when dealing with figures with large numbers of zeros, and in stories involving percentages, when the figures often did not add up to one hundred.

Considerable effort was made by the Duiwaibu to check that official statistics had been accurately represented, although their veracity was the responsibility of the source. Official figures often originated with the various ministries and other central government sources. However, where figures came from less important organs of state or from further afield, the commitment to verification declined. Thus, production figures claimed by a commune or factory a long way from Beijing, and perhaps reported by a Xinhua branch or by the local press in the first instance, tended either to be reproduced as they were, contradictions and all, or were considered to be too confusing and were simply discarded. Here again, the level of skill and application of the journalist was the relevant factor, rather than any political consideration.

These observations must invite speculation about the degree of specialization among journalists at Xinhua, and about the extent of their professional training. In the Duiwaibu, although there were exceptions, the majority of journalists in 1979 had no particular skills relevant to the section and to the type of work to which they were assigned, and any facility with the material that they were able to develop came from being on the job. All too often, the only requirement had been some ability in English or in one of the other languages in which Duiwaibu material appeared. Moreover, many journalists had been seconded to the Duiwaibu from other jobs at various times, with little reference to either their aptitude or their inclination to do the work. Thus there were on the staff people who had set out to be teachers, or linguists, but had found themselves at the news agency; the element of free choice was lost, and enthusiasm accordingly diminished.

News policy over the years had not favoured specialization or differentiation of tasks among journalists, and a too-rigid interpretation of the injunction to loyalty to the party further reduced the scope for the journalist to develop special skills or to exercise his initiative. The result had been an outflow of news from the Duiwaibu that was, for the size and resources of the Xinhua organization, both low in volume and very uneven in quality. The journalism training centre, established in Beijing in 1978 with foreign assistance, had only just begun to redress some of these problems, but would in future years raise questions unequivocally about the role of the journalist in China which to this day remain unanswered (see Chapter 2).

As a determinant of the shape of the Duiwaibu's news about China, a few words must be said about the attitudes of the journalists themselves. First, what was the attitude of the journalists to their readers? How much did Duiwaibu staff know and understand of the world outside and how it received their work?

11

LIVERPOOL JOHN MOORES UNIVERSITY
Higher .... L.R.C.
TEL. 0151 231 3701/3634

The world beyond China's frontiers provided the Duiwaibu with some feedback, since the Research Section regularly monitored pick-up of Duiwaibu stories in foreign press organs, concentrating on those which took the most material from the Xinhua wire at that time, notably the *South China Morning Post* in Hong Kong, the *Far Eastern Economic Review*, Agence France Presse, United Press International, Associated Press, Reuters, *Time Magazine* and *Newsweek*. Also, individual journalists monitored for their own satisfaction the extent to which the stories from their section of the Duiwaibu found their way into the foreign press. Yet there was little evidence to suggest that these indications of the relative newsworthiness of items were analysed in any systematic way so as to target the reporting and writing up of news specifically for foreign consumption.

In truth, in 1979, journalists of the Duiwaibu still lived largely in isolation from the realities of the world outside China. There was no direct contact between the Duiwaibu and its foreign readers, nor had press conferences yet been implemented for foreign correspondents based in China. Of the journalists working for the Duiwaibu, only a few had seen service abroad, or had the opportunity to go abroad for study. Many had matured in the years during and after the Cultural Revolution, when knowledge of the world beyond China's frontiers was little valued, and indeed was sometimes regarded with suspicion – an attitude that had not entirely disappeared. It is not surprising, therefore, that the average journalist found it hard to comprehend the world of his reader, or to conceptualize events in China from the foreign readers' point of view.

Reinforcing this lack of awareness was a tradition of ethnocentrism stretching back millennia. This manifested itself in the Duiwaibu in a practical way as an unstated assumption on the part of some journalists that it was not necessary to modify the technique and idiom of newswriting to match the conceptual categories of the non-Chinese world. In other words, the foreign reader could take it or leave it. This tendency was reflected both in the type of material chosen for news stories and in the way that the material was treated.

The other dimension of the question of the journalists' attitudes concerned their motivation, or their attitude toward the Duiwaibu itself.

In this connection, the problem of most pressing importance in 1979, and one that had a profound impact on the morale of staff working throughout the Duiwaibu, was the quite apparent neglect of talent. This was evident in the relatively high average age of the organization's leading cadres, in the sidetracking and failure to exploit the full potential of promising younger staff members, and in the retention in critical middle-management positions of a few cadres who consistently blocked constructive change.

The problem was partly one of adherence to rules of seniority in situations in which younger men and women might actually do the job better, a human dilemma by no means unique to China. It was also partly as a result of tensions and suspicions of a political nature, which were a hangover from the period of the Cultural Revolution, and an inclination to trust only those people who most obviously and uncritically supported the party line. Needless to say, such people were not always the most competent, and nor were they necessarily the most genuine in their patriotism or in their support for China's stated goal of socialist modernization.

The lack of a clear career path within Xinhua, with tangible rewards for achievement, combined with political constraints on professionalism to demotivate many of the brightest young members of staff in the Duiwaibu. This more than anything encouraged the exodus to *China Daily*, where the hope existed for a time at least that a good job could be done, and that talent would be recognized.

Structural factors

There are finally a number of structural factors, concerned with the nature of the organization and the way in which it functioned, that influenced the Duiwaibu's effectiveness as a conduit for news about China. Chief among these were: communication within the organization; the degree of consultation; the pace of work expected of journalists; and the level of technology in force in 1979.

Communication within the Duiwaibu on matters of substance was not what might have been expected in an organization that had as its purpose the publication of information. Among the political, economic and cultural sections of the Duiwaibu there was little formal collaboration, although there was a good deal of informal contact between individual members of the sections. There appeared to be no strategy in place to coordinate work in different sections that was on related themes, in spite of the planning that went on within sections and higher up. Nor were there any bridging articles to help the reader relate material covered by one section to that covered by another.

Final choice of the balance of political, economic, cultural and other stories was left to the editor for the day, who was responsible to his superiors, and especially to the head of the Duiwaibu. As noted above, important themes to be covered were determined by meetings of senior journalists within the Duiwaibu. However, beyond this important core material, the editor's choice seemed as much as anything to be determined by whatever each section had managed to complete in the course of the day.

Nor did the daily work-team normally confer very much with journalists working in the different sections. On occasions, the work-team, in lighting on a particular theme for the morning – perhaps taking as a text an article from the morning's *People's Daily* – would pre-empt a theme on which one of the sections had been working for several days. On one occasion in my experience, members of one section complained bitterly that the work-team for that day had 'used up all the news'. The lack of communication between the work-team and the regular sections on the allocation of tasks and deadlines not infrequently posed problems of this kind.

A similar gap in communication existed between the Duiwaibu in Beijing and the Xinhua branches throughout China on which the Duiwaibu relied for part of its output. Although broad directives about the sort of material required were issued by Head Office to the branches, and stories were sent in by wire or, in less urgent cases, through the post, communication between the Duiwaibu and the branches was haphazard at the best of times. Even branches in major centres, such as Shanghai, Nanjing or Guangzhou, failed to communicate in a way that was anywhere near satisfactory. If communication within Xinhua was flawed in this way, how much consultation on decision-making could be expected to exist?

Surprisingly, there were in fact pockets of consultation, if not actual participation in the running of the Duiwaibu. Informally and *within* each section, there was discussion about the allocation of work, the approach to be adopted to particular material, deadlines, staff rotas and other work details. Although authority usually rested in the end with one person, the views of other members of staff were often taken into account. Within the Duiwaibu as a whole, meetings were held both to consult staff on administrative matters and to pass on the decisions of the leadership.

Consultation did not mean any more than that, however, and was generally restricted to the implementation rather than the formulation of policy. Delegation of authority on important matters did not really exist; whether it was editorial policy, modernization of equipment, provision of training or strategic planning of the agency's work, the most senior journalists, all party members, took the decisions. This fact made many of the younger staff of the Duiwaibu feel that the leadership of the organization for which they worked was impenetrable and remote.

Some attention must be given to the pace of work at the Duiwaibu, the speed with which news stories were compiled and released. Although the daily work-teams functioned much as journalists do in the West – dealing with important items of news as they came up, and meeting strict deadlines according to which even minutes lost are considered unacceptable – the great majority of journalists, i.e. those not chosen for the work-team, were under no pressure, and what was not finished one day could be finished the next, or the day after that. It is not surprising, therefore, that the Duiwaibu often found itself beaten to the post on items of Chinese news picked up by foreign correspondents and news agencies from the domestic Chinese press.

Already by 1979, the days when foreigners resident in Beijing could not read the Chinese press, or were unable to obtain copies of national and provincial newspapers, had gone. The pace of news work at the Duiwaibu had not yet caught up to this fact, and it was still not uncommon for an editor to brood on a piece of news for several days before either killing it or deciding to put it out on the wire. The pace of its work clearly set the Duiwaibu apart from news agencies elsewhere.

A few words are necessary about the level of equipment at the

Duiwaibu. On the whole the equipment in place in 1979 – the typewriters, some of the printing presses, the Xinhua teleprinters provided for foreign correspondents in Beijing, and the single photocopier shared by the whole of the Duiwaibu – was relatively primitive. A start had been made on the acquisition of more modern technology, however, and half a dozen word processors made their appearance in the course of the year.

In my view, the level of technology employed mattered less at the time than the horizons of Duiwaibu staff. A greater number of dictionaries, style manuals and foreign books on journalism would have helped far more, as would an increase in the number of subscriptions to foreign newspapers and in the time permitted to journalists to read them. All these things in fact came with the passage of time, although the political culture of Xinhua, which in ensuing years did not change all that much, may in the event have determined the use to which they could be put.

Conclusion

In seeking to promote through its national news media the most favourable view possible of its achievements, the Chinese government is not unlike many other national governments engaged in the debate on freedom of the press that has been taking place for some years within Unesco. There is, however, an additional element in the Chinese case that has to do with the orthodox Chinese attitude to the concept of criticism.

If, as Mao would have it, contradictions may be resolved through debate, and one may thereby arrive at a correct understanding of a situation and of the course of action that it warrants, then further criticism, or insistence on a divergent point of view, must be seen either as the result of imperfect understanding or as an act of fundamental betrayal. Criticism may in certain circumstances be seen to be 'counter-revolutionary', and the scope for critical or investigative journalism is correspondingly reduced. Thus, although Deng Xiaoping may have exhorted people to seek truth from facts, the penalties for actually doing so, where the party has made up its mind about an issue, may be severe.

This raises both the question of whether the journalist can divorce himself from the events going on around him, inside and outside his country, and by implication the broader issue of the role of journalism under socialism. There is no doubt that there are many issues on which the committed journalist must feel strongly, and some on which he may completely disagree with established policy. Can the journalist's task as it is perceived in the West – one of investigation, exposition and persuasion – coexist with the four principles of adherence to the socialist road, the dictatorship of the proletariat, the leadership of the communist party, and acceptance of Marxism, Leninism, Mao Tse-tung thought?

Certainly in recent years there has been a discernible tendency on the part of some Chinese journalists, not only within the Duiwaibu, to attempt to report more objectively on a whole range of subjects alongside statements of policy. Certainly the contradiction between simple propaganda and more complex news is bound to become more apparent as journalists become better educated and more professional. However, until the government and the Chinese Communist Party are able to absorb and benefit from criticism and from the objective reporting of negative conditions, it is likely that constraints will continue to hamper the development of the news function, as opposed to the propaganda function, of the national news agency and all other organs of the press.

LIVERPOOL JOHN MOORES UNIVERSITY
LEARNING SERVICES

2
Pioneering Xinhua's International Journalism Training Centre

JOHN DAVID

The scope of the task

In 1979, the Thomson Foundation was asked by the then Ministry of Propaganda of the People's Republic of China (PRC) to help set up *China Daily*, the first English-language daily paper in that country since 1949. It was probably envy of the success of this – the paper within a year was usurping Xinhua News Agency as the major news source for world outlets – that led to a proposal in 1984 that Xinhua and Thomson should establish an international journalism training centre at their Xuanwumen Xidajie central compound in Beijing, to improve the news selection and news processing standards of the agency's 600 English-language journalists.

This was an important project from two particular standpoints: Xinhua is by far the biggest and most influential news organization in the PRC, and has the status of a ministry, while the Thomson Foundation, although a small organization, has had 25 years of experience in trying to improve media outlets in the developing world, and is therefore adept at working under any form of government.

For the just curious or the China-watcher alike, the language of the country offers a serious hurdle. Newspapers do not provide a source of information unless the reader has 1,500 characters, and even then it is what appears between the columns that is significant. That is why the establishment of *China Daily* was so important. Prior to that, the only news conduits for nonlinguists were Xinhua's poorly constructed and dogma-ridden foreign-language service, and the equally inadequate, officially dominated and even less topical periodicals, such as the weekly *Beijing Review*.

English? Yes, even the reluctant Francophones regard the English language as essential in the world news flow. An appeal by the Thomson Foundation for financial backing from the Overseas Development Administration (ODA) of the British Foreign and Commonwealth Office was thus successful. Presumably they spotted the political capital to be made, although the foundation's staff were reminded of the need to remain uncompromised in this regard. Xinhua – known in some parts as the New China News Agency – is central to all news read, heard or watched in China, since no other news organ has representation in every part of the country. Nor, with the exception of *Renmin Ribao* (*People's Daily*) and *Guangming Daily* (the intellectuals' paper), are they represented overseas. Therefore virtually all non-local news in China is Xinhua-orientated, and almost all news about China read externally is inspired (if that be the word) by Xinhua reportage.

Xinhua has a payroll of 6,500 (compared with the 1,200 of Reuter, Britain's external news agency). It has 100 bureaux around the world (Reuter 35), offices in all provinces and autonomous regions except Taiwan, and transmits in English, French, Spanish, Arabic and Russian, as well as in Chinese. It also has more than twenty publications, with subjects ranging from the economy to photography and sport. Apart from the printed daily news bulletin in each of its languages, the most important publication is *Reference News*. In 1981 the circulation of *Reference News* was nine million copies a day, but is now down to half that. The decline is said to be as a result of alternative sources of information becoming available. The publication comes in three grades. The first is for general consumption, while the second is restricted to middle-rank cadres. Most interesting is the third grade. This goes only to top-ranking government and party personnel and diplomats. It carries extracts from articles in the foreign media which may well contain the truth, but which are felt to be undesirable for the eyes of ordinary people.

Xinhua's titular head was Director-General Mu Qing (a son of whom was a diligent pupil of mine). But the effective controller at the time was Guo Chaoren, a 45-ish practical ex-reporter who, unfortunately, speaks

Russian but no English. In putting down the benchmarks for the centre's training, Guo gave every indication of a liberal attitude. Indeed, ridding the agency as much as possible from the shackles of communist ideology seemed to be a prerequisite of his stated ambition to head an agency to rank alongside the big four – Associated Press, United Press International, Agence France Press and Reuter. The crucial question at the time, with sweeping political and journalistic connotations, was: Does Xinhua wish to remain the eyes, ears and mouth of the Chinese Communist Party? Put bluntly, does Xinhua continue to toe the Marxist line that what goes in newspapers is what motivates the masses behind the party? Or was there to be a sea change, with truth the criteria for good news or bad? He was unequivocal. Xinhua was aiming in the next decade to be one of the Big Five. Credibility was everything. Therefore news was fact, whether it suited the party or not. And all staff were being so instructed. (It should perhaps be noted that, in the post-Tiananmen era, both Mu and Guo have been 'under official observation' because of their professional conduct during the student unrest.)

Getting to grips

For a newcomer, the shock on seeing the appointed lecture rooms, newly adapted for the use of the Thomson-Xinhua centre alone, was considerable. Rigidity pervaded all. Straight rows of desks, tall crib screens, a podium, all presented with pride and all militating against the aura of professional informality that is normally aimed at.

An aural English test – well, a cosy chat, really – had been used to avoid the embarrassment of complete lack of communication in the centre. We were, after all, setting out to give a technical skill in a second language. We did not ask for fluency, only understanding. Despite this initial earlier contact, not a flicker of recognition came from those pioneers when the instructors crossed to the podium and its battery of microphones and tape recorders. We were to learn much about those students and those microphones.

One of the group was to say later: 'On that first day we sat up straight, eyes ahead, and waited. We expected you to come in, wait until you had all our attention, give your lecture, gather up your papers, and go.' That is precisely what the instructors did not do, even if that is what was expected from lecturers in Chinese universities. Discussion, even argument, became the drill, not unquestioning acceptance of old men's wisdom.

Those microphones? 'Just to record your comments, so we can use them for other groups', we were assured by the authorities. One instructor, prone to waiving his arms about in animated discussion, one day knocked a microphone to the floor. 'Oh dear, that'll give the secret police a headache', he joked. At the end of the session – a mere fifteen seconds after the first student had left the room – the Chinese director of the centre shot in from her office, looking anxious. 'There are no secret police', she said soothingly, without the slightest preamble. 'We just want a record for the future.' Perhaps there was no eavesdropping by Big Brother. But we noted how quickly the mention of such a possibility within the four walls of the lecture room provoked a defensive reaction without.

Tuition systems at the training centre varied little from those built up from a quarter of a century's experience of news tuition for people using English, often not their first language. The participants, each one of whom had learned English from a Chinese who had never left its shores, were predictably diligent and good-humoured. There were no disciplinary problems, and lots of laughter. Often we crossed cultural boundaries. We encouraged close and persistent questioning, even of government or party functionaries. Bad news was good news in a news sense, news values paramount. When it came to writing, it was predominantly a case of what to leave out, such as flowery phrases derived directly from their tongue, and clichés. An anti-favourite among these, for example, was 'building stronger bilateral ties' to describe, with never a variation, the purpose of meetings between national VIPs.

Individually most of the students lapped this up. After all, they did not lack intelligence; Xinhua has always been able to cream off China's best graduates, particularly those with language aptitude. This is because of the country's former system of assignment to jobs, with the seniority of the news agency as a work unit an attraction and the chance of an overseas assignment a bonus. Politically we were frank, and were greeted by frankness in return. When they asked about Western systems, the answers were as honest as could be given; and they told their instructors of their problems. It was easy to become a father confessor, because Chinese emotion, although instinctively well hidden, is powerful when unearthed.

The students in general demonstrated one particular trait setting them apart from their Western counterparts: gullibility. Whereas young Western journalists quickly acquire a veneer of cynicism, this quality was rarely present in the Chinese students, at least in public. Perhaps this was a reflection of their education, portraying life as a series of cast-iron rights and wrongs. Whatever the case, it proved a trap for the unwary tutor. Realism has to be an aim for a vocational trainer restricted mainly to a lecture-room environment, otherwise there is an inevitable slide into academia. We tried to present realistic news situations to the students as often as possible. One day, therefore, a willing Canadian was pressed into service at a simulated news conference. He was briefed to be a US naval press officer announcing that a combat aircraft from a carrier had crashed into the sea 40 miles off Shanghai, armed with a nuclear warhead. It was fiction, of course.

The following morning the 'captain' reported to the centre and, eager to do his duty, had scrounged from somewhere a genuine US navy cap and a portmanteau of facts and statistics about the aircraft and its deployment. He spelled all this out to the trainees, who were agog. They conscientiously noted the tiniest details. Then, at the close of the conference and over coffee, one came to me and whispered: 'That was real, wasn't it?' A horrible possibility dawned. The group was hushed and an announcement made that 'of course' the exercise has been simulated. But then it was discovered that two of the group had skipped the break and were now back in their newsrooms working on the big story. Shortly it would be transmitted to the world. We headed off this dreadful scenario in time, thus averting, possibly, a major world incident. On reflection, we had not properly appreciated that to the average Chinese mind a foreign expert, plus impressive statistics, plus a uniform, added up plainly to authority. And authority is to be believed, without caveat.

One of our prime responsibilities was to widen the news selection skill of our young charges. Any keen reader of the Chinese press will confirm that the delight of most writers is the official line, and that delight turns to delirium if statistics are plentiful. So we gave non-stop encouragement to reporters to try to beat official sources to a newsbreak. This initiative was taken up with gusto by many of them. But the challenge, the lifeblood of Western news gathering, did not seem always to survive the transition from lecture room to the real Chinese world, hardly surprisingly.

Even the most innocuous of stories could receive the official squelch. During my incumbency, the movement to free markets was gaining momentum, with peasants bypassing the centralized marketing structure to the benefit, apparently, of both themselves and their city customers. Several quite lively versions of this sociologically important story were written by young reporters on assignment from our centre. After completing our course, one feature writer floated the idea of an article along those lines for international dissemination by his own department. 'Yes, yes', responded his editor. 'We can tell how prosperous the peasants are becoming. But make sure you start off the feature by outlining the party policy and quoting Deng Xiaoping – we don't want our Western friends jumping to the wrong idea that we are dumping Marxism.' The feature never did get written for external consumption.

Rumours of the informality of our training attitudes spread like wildfire. There was, and probably still is, some reluctance to take the Thomson course, since most of those qualified would much prefer to go abroad for instruction. But 50 participants went through the system in the first year, and this was doubled in the second, and the UK organization assigned four instructors instead of the original three. Significantly, Xinhua then asked that a course for senior personnel, foreign bureaux managers, desk editors and the like, should be instituted.

Whereas the basic courses dealt with news appreciation, reporting techniques – such as interviewing and story construction, feature writing and copy editing – the senior editors and managers were led into more philosophical considerations, such as bureau organization, staffing and staff relationships, and the selection of locations for new bureaux. Both grades of courses continue, surviving the crisis of June 1989. At the time of the crisis, the two instructors were hurriedly evacuated on advice from the British Embassy. It was the Xinhua authorities who, after a decent interval, beckoned for the team to return. They went back after six months.

The difficulty with training is that its benefits are impossible to quantify. Yet the question must be addressed on how effective was (or is, since it is continuing) the effort made. Was there any impact, or was the whole thing an exercise in window-dressing?

The limits of change

Events in Tiananmen Square in June 1989 proved that the leadership of China had not the slightest intention of making a quantum leap politically, and thus that journalism in China was not overnight to be translated into a fearless quest for the truth in the name of the reader. Indeed, for some of the individuals who went through our particular mill, the path ahead – even prior to the uprising – was quite clear.

Shortly after completing our course with its recommendation to be both persistent and fair in fact-finding, one of the students heard he was to be posted to Zimbabwe as a correspondent for Xinhua. An instructor who had worked as a journalist several times in that southern African country offered to pass on tips and some press contacts to the young man, who was going overseas for the first time. He seemed doubtful when presented with the contacts list; Xinhua journalists rarely, at that time at least, made contact with their fellow correspondents from other countries. But he did not hesitate when dealing with one question: 'What would you do', he was asked by his former tutor, 'if you found evidence that Zimbabwean soldiers had carried out tribal killings?' His reply: 'Nothing'. Why not? 'Because my government is friendly with the Zimbabwean government and I would not try to do anything which might upset that.'

From our vantage point, then, a failure. None of our exhortations to find and record the truth seem to have entered this man's consciousness. He was a party functionary to the end, certainly beyond our encouragement and example. Which, after all, was his right. The hope was that not all the minds loaned to us were quite so unyielding, and that a tiny seed is there, dormant like a poppy, to flower perhaps decades hence.

Most of the course work was aimed at improving the international services of Xinhua. There was some evidence that the agency was becoming a more speedy and reliable source of news in its world service, although none would claim Thomson techniques to be solely credited. The norms of news-gathering in terms of timeliness have certainly improved. For example, in late 1988 there was an earthquake near Kunming measuring 9.4 on the Richter scale. The first Xinhua flash was received in Beijing inside four hours – not bad, considering the remoteness of the epicentre – and only a stupid human error prevented the world knowing inside eight hours. Contrast this with the party's news blackout that has stopped the world, even now, from appreciating the magnitude of the quake that destroyed Tangshan city in July 1976. In terms of human suffering, this was possibly the most destructive tremor ever, with 800,000 officially dead or injured and the probable toll nearer 1,370,000.

Equally telling, given subsequent events, was that Xinhua was the first to report the initial civil disturbances in Llasa four years ago, before the party apparatus clamped down on Tibet. So we have some evidence that Xinhua, in news terms, was becoming a more speedy and professional source of news within its own borders.

When I was in Tanzania in 1989, working with that country's Shigata News Agency, I had an unsolicited testimonial to the Chinese agency's improving world status. Since Reuter decline to supply the country with any more wire copy until the bill is paid, Xinhua is the sole source of international news for the Tanzanian media. Worries about this brought a reassuring response from the managing editor of the English-language national newspaper. He said: 'Xinhua has much improved in the past five years, both in breadth of coverage and quality of news writing.'

One reason for delays within Xinhua is certainly political control. A senior editor checks everything for political sensitivity after the staff, including foreign 'polishers' – revise sub-editors who correct the language – have done their part. But how does the senior editor keep abreast of his or her role? When the Thomson-Xinhua centre started up, Western staff announced that they wished to work a five-day week. Knowing that the Chinese work on Saturdays, a sticking-point was anticipated. Not so; the students have to attend meetings on Saturdays anyway. The centre's premises are opposite rooms occupied by Xinhua's Research Department. From time to time these rooms were full, people overflowing on to chairs in the corridor. Chinese was being spoken, but what were these meetings about? It transpired that they were political. At mandatory sessions, all staff, including those temporarily in the centre's care, are told of the party's attitude to events of the day or week, or situations coming up, such as a party congress. As one insider put it: 'So we know what our duty is'.

In a hierarchical society, of course, censorship of self is the most pernicious form, and is at its worst in China. Each strata strives to keep its record clean. So words, phrases and facts are taken out in case they offend the party level above. Within Xinhua there is even a system of personal fines, deducted from bonuses, for staff who make errors, including errors of political judgment. So there is, beyond all doubt, no single Mr Censor sitting with blue pencil poised in Xinhua. How could there be? Shifting news copy on a world scale is a mammoth, 24-hour operation. No single person could read everything in Chinese, let alone the other languages of transmission.

June 1989 changed many things. But, prior to that, there were some encouraging signs that the clammy hand of party bureaucracy was lifting a little. Those Saturday morning briefings, which lasted three hours or longer in 1985, were often cancelled, or occupied only a half-hour by 1988. It is believed, unofficially, that just 10 per cent of Xinhua staff are party members. One young man applying for membership said candidly that he was doing so only 'as career insurance'. He did not believe the ideology.

Within four weeks of the training centre starting up, a 28-year-old reporter asked if she might tell a staff member a secret. She glanced round to see who might be overhearing, then announced vehemently: 'I hate communism. I hate it. It doesn't work.' So much for a childhood of brainwashing, red bows in her hair, and thoughts of Chairman Mao. Few of the others were quite so outspoken, although they were much more prone to be so with an understanding foreigner than with other Chinese.

Conformity permeates lives and culture, so the minds of young Chinese reporters proved far more fettered than those of young Western journalists, and new concepts were less speedily grasped. One effect was their relative inability to frame probing questions. They have, after all, little opportunity to practice. Weighing opposing theories also comes with difficulty to young people used to having only the 'correct' version put to them.

As a result, news gathering in the PRC amounts to little more than waiting for official news releases and comments. The party offers little chance, normally, to any but a handful of favoured journalists to query statements, statistics or policies outlined. At times it could be dangerous for reporters to harass a spokesman of any official establishment. 'Was it you who annoyed the minister with your silly questions?' would be the charge, and the penalty could be serious. Hence journalists are receivers of alleged facts, never hunters.

A partial exception was *China Daily*, which from the start tried to report honestly while still perforce remaining firmly within the system. This philosophy was adopted, founder editor Feng Xiliang told me, on the grounds that its foreign readership was much more attuned to revelation and much less likely to swallow straight propaganda than Chinese readers. They would be more likely to spot 'officialese' which cloaked inaccuracy or half-truth, so causing lack of credibility in the newspaper.

The man in question is a journalism hero. Educated in part at an American journalism school, he created a technically acceptable daily newspaper that constantly crossed the powers that be when it came to frankness in its choice of stories, despite being in principle conceived and backed by these powers. Typical were stories involving corruption among party leaders, albeit generally low-level ones. This editor once told me that he was retiring early. 'I am exhausted. I have been carpeted once too often', he explained. He said that in the early days, and during periods of political tension, he had to report to the Minister of Information on average four times a week to explain real or imagined transgressions. His replacement, once a Thomson Foundation student in London, is a much less cavalier character, which may explain the comparative dullness of the publication today.

This mention of government intervention leads into the question of

Chinese government information services. Or, more correctly, the absence of them. Certainly even Xinhua suffers from the dearth of channels of communication from central sources. The system is at its worst with the publication, in quasi-legal form, of new legislation. No attempt has been made to sound out public opinion or to sample feedback. Zhongnanhai remains in blissful ignorance of the general mood, and this breeds the brand of panic manifested in Tiananmen Square.

A conclusion must be that better government media relations are a prerequisite and part and parcel of any real tilt towards democracy in the PRC. Xinhua is central to any such change, because at the moment if Xinhua says it then all know that it is the party saying it. There have been some quavering steps towards independence for China's print media. There are about 1,700 newspapers and 4,100 magazines registered in the country, 57 of them classified as nationwide publications. Not included in this array, yet of considerable philosophical importance, are the 'unhealthy tabloids', underground sheets that carry mainly fairy stories about past and present politicians and their supposedly lurid personal peccadillos.

Naturally these are unpopular with officialdom, which periodically cracks down. Something of the scale of this aberration comes in a *China Daily* report in 1985, which said 50 of them had been forcibly closed down. This is periodically repeated. Yet it has been estimated that there were still 400 of these publications circulating in Beijing alone at one time, although the cover price was up to ten times that of the normal printed news outlets. So the public likes them, presumably as a change from the turgid government line. But then the government itself, instead of just railing against the underground sheets, could have stamped on all of them, instantly, by denying them newsprint, which is in genuinely short supply. This is not done. Why? Could they provide a necessary safety valve? Is this dimly recognized at party headquarters?

One time party General Secretary Hu Yaobang once outlined the basic requirement from the media. He stipulated 80 per cent 'good news' and 20 per cent 'revealing, instructive and interesting'. But he also said publicly that news organs should serve the public as well as the party. During his time, there were some minor moves towards liberalization.

Professor Wang Zhong of Fudan University, Shanghai, was set to head a Press Commission to suggest a way ahead for China's media by 1990. The fate of this report is unknown to the writer. One of its widely touted recommendations was that each organ, though remaining in government orbit, should have an editor who alone should be responsible for editorial content. Hence it should no longer be the prerogative of the party to decide whether a story suited or conformed to policy.

Like so many aspects of life in the PRC, the commission and its report is probably in abeyance, awaiting the passing of the years and personalities. Chinese history goes back 3,000 years, so China-watchers should not be in too much of a hurry. Certain it is that one small group of foreign journalism trainers will not have made any fundamental changes in the short time since China's 'opening up'. But, if there is among some of its practitioners an awakened sense of fairness, and if the words 'balance' and 'impartiality' are applied to some of Xinhua's news reporting, then this should be regarded as reward enough.

3

Changes of line at 'China Daily': fluctuating party policy or fluctuating control?

JEAN CONLEY AND STEPHEN TRIPOLI

On the outside even while inside

For a variety of political, cultural and historical reasons that are not within the scope of this study, the Chinese can be reticent with foreigners, including those in their midst. In times of political crises, such as those surrounding the pro-democracy demonstrations of 1986-7 and 1989, this is even more apparent. It should therefore seem a small irony only to those not familiar with China that we learned more in recent months about what was going on at *China Daily* during a crisis for which we were present – the first one mentioned above – than we did while we were there. Time and the physical distance, combined with the ability to talk privately to some of the individuals involved, produced candor about both crises. This chapter is the result of those conversations, combined with what was known about the situation in China.

This is almost exclusively an eyewitness account of the changing patterns of coverage of those crises by the newspaper *China Daily*, showing why the coverage fluctuated as it did. What happened at *China Daily* during those days is indicative of a situation that has greater significance for China than merely affecting the state of journalism there.

This is not a formal academic paper. It is rather a combined research paper and news account, with all references contained in the text. The chapter will first look in detail at *what* the coverage was in *China Daily* during these two periods, then will look at *why* it evolved that way, and finally will outline the larger implications.

China Daily is an English-language newspaper with a circulation of about 100,000 – *China Daily* says it is closer to 150,000, but one knowledgeable staff member disputed that. In less than seven years, it has become one of the major voices to the outside world of the People's Republic of China (PRC). It offers same-day publication in several parts of the world, via satellite link from its Beijing headquarters to printing plants in Shanghai, Hong Kong, London and New York.

We worked at *China Daily* from the middle of 1986 to the middle of 1987 as 'polishers', or what would be known in Britain as sub-editors and in the United States as copy editors. The work involved regular participation in the daily editorial meeting, although polishers had virtually no influence on, and often little knowledge of, decisions involving the most sensitive matters.

The 1986-7 student demonstrations, and the campaign against 'bourgeois liberalization'

Ignoring the news

On 10 December 1986, the *New York Times,* inside its front section (page 9), quoted a report by Japan's Kyodo News Service of anti-government demonstrations by several thousand students in Hefei, capital of Anhui province. The story pre-dated, by nearly two weeks, any even oblique mention in *China Daily* of student demonstrations. But an after-the-crisis propaganda booklet, published by *Beijing Review* and titled 'Student Unrest: What Is It All About?', outlined unrest on several campuses as a genesis of that year's demonstrations, starting at least a full month before even the *New York Times* account.

The Times followed with a 14 December story, also inside the front section (page 13), which stated that students of Beijing University had put up posters on campus calling for more democracy. The story added that thousands of students were said to have demonstrated in the provinces, also calling for democracy. A page 1 lead story on 21 December spoke of thousands of students marching in Shanghai, demanding democracy and press freedom; of wall-posters appearing in Beijing calling for greater freedom; and of the Xinhua News Agency's first acknowledgment of the demonstrations, an interview with an unidentified education official.

The following day, with coverage again in *The Times, China Daily* ran a single story, below the fold on page 1. It was the interview with the unnamed official cited in the previous day's *Times*, headlined 'It's legal if students demonstrate – official'. Answering four questions, the official alluded to demonstrations around the country and said that they would not be suppressed as long as they didn't violate the law. He also took note of the wall-posters and reiterated that such unsigned material had been outlawed in 1980. (In fairness, the thirteen-hour time difference may have made this story roughly simultaneous with *The Times'* 21 December coverage.)

Coverage in *The Times* rose to the forefront at this point and remained there for several weeks, with frequent page 1 stories, numerous accompanying pieces, analyses, commentary and photos. In the final week of December, *The Times* reported major demonstrations in Chinese cities, plus rioting, intentional blockages of traffic, defiance of government bans on demonstrations, and government denunciations of the demonstrators. *China Daily*, after a slow start, chose to report just one of those aspects.

The 'misguided agitators' phase

In *China Daily*, the next mention came on 24 December, again below the fold on page 1, in a story headlined 'Extreme action affects stability'. The article quoted at some length an editorial on that theme which had appeared in the leading newspaper *People's Daily*, and made no direct mention of any demonstrations. This set a pattern for the next phase of coverage, the 'misguided agitators' phase.

On 25 December, an editorial quoted Jiang Zemin, who was then mayor of Shanghai (and rose to become general secretary of the Chinese Communist Party and chairman of the Central Military Commission, perhaps China's most powerful leader), as pointing out that 'patriotic students ... should guard against the instigation of an extremely small number of people who are stirring up trouble'.

The next day, the opinion page reprinted a *People's Daily* commentary, 'Anarchism is not democracy', warning that 'Anyone who favours political reform, young students included' should beware of causing a

Cultural Revolution-style calamity 'to repeat itself under any slogan, however beautiful-sounding'.

The lead story on 29 December, headlined 'Unrest is blamed on "lawless elements"', quoted a *People's Daily* account of student demonstrations in Nanjing, which reported that 'a few "lawless troublemakers" started to damage cars, destroy shop fronts, beat up people, insult women and throw bundles of burning rice straw'.

On 31 December, another lead story quoted the vice-minister of the State Education Commission, He Dongchan, as drawing 'a clear distinction between those students who were patriotically showing their enthusiasm for reforms and a few non-students who had committed offenses against the constitution'.

This type of reporting continued into mid-January 1987; reports repeatedly spoke of non-students sneaking into demonstrations to stir up anti-government feelings, 'rabble rousers' and the like. Near the end of the first week in January, the term 'bourgeois liberalization' – sometimes also called 'complete Westernization' – appeared for the first time as a label for what the misguided were advocating. Dissident Fang Lizhi also surfaced as a culprit, which incited students when his removal as vice-president of the Chinese University of Science and Technology in Hefei was announced, on page 1, on 13 January.

At *China Daily* during this period, foreigners saw obvious signs of ferment, and even turmoil. Younger staff members were appearing with excited accounts of demonstrations in Beijing, which many foreigners witnessed as well. The situation was at the heart of daily discussion. Mid-level editors, asked at *China Daily's* news desk why these demonstrations were receiving no coverage, would give predictable, if sometimes sheepish, answers: there really were very few demonstrators, it really was not important, those involved were very young, etc.

But questions of coverage were also being debated at *China Daily* outside the presence of foreigners, and in the charged atmosphere it emerged that the communist party hierarchy was itself divided, and one source of anxiety was that, with factions forming above, media leaders were unsure of whose lead they should follow.

One foreigner encountered a young *China Daily* editor, sitting alone at the news desk late one night, his face creased in thought. What would happen in the party's power struggle? he was asked, to which he shook his head and replied that no one could tell, and that no one could ever tell in these circumstances, and that that was the problem. This dilemma would be felt by the Chinese even more painfully two and a half years later, in the summer of 1989.

There was some factual coverage of what was happening during this period, mostly embedded in other stories referred to here. The 25 December story cited above, for instance, contains quite a bit of information on demonstrations, and where and when they had occurred. Looking back at those stories, however, it appears that most of the facts were released to service propaganda objectives, and particularly to stress that students were motivated only by high ideals, that the activity was a threat to the nation's stability, and that, despite everything, the situation was under control and reform was proceeding. This last point was emphasized repeatedly from mid-January and throughout the remainder of the crisis.

The fall of Hu Yaobang, and a propaganda typhoon

China Daily trailed no one in its page 1 announcement, on 17 January, of the fall of Hu Yaobang as general secretary of the communist party Central Committee. Zhao Ziyang succeeded him. With the party's upper-level power struggle resolved, China Daily marched resolutely to the new tune of the Propaganda Ministry, which is responsible for media affairs and answers directly to the party's Central Committee. This tune had two themes. First, a reassurance to the world that reform and the policy of opening to the West would continue (the New York Times also reported the day after Hu's ouster – as did other media inside and outside China – that both Zhao and Deng Xiaoping had personally assured a continuation of the open policy), while reassuring people at home and abroad that no sweeping purge would occur. And, second, an incessant drumbeat of propaganda over the next month that characterized student demonstrators as well-meaning, but utterly misguided. The between-semesters break that fell at this time was used as the basis for many stories of students returning to their home areas and, after deep thought and labour with the masses, realizing the error of their ways.

For example, on 19 January, the national news page (page 3) quoted from a *China Youth News* report of how nearly 10,000 students in the capital would provide services in urban and rural areas during vacation. 'This activity ... aims at helping young people understand society, learn to respect others, and strengthen their concept to serve the people, an official said.' On 3 February, a story stated that 'After a recent survey, students found they need to know more about themselves and society in general.'

On 17 February, Li Peng, then a vice-premier and minister in charge of education, called for 'more opportunities for college students to experience real life outside their colleges', plus better ideological training. He added that most students had good intentions, but that a few 'under the influence of bourgeois liberalization ... still hold some wrong ideas'.

Toward the end of the vacation period, a headline proclaimed that the 'vacation matured students' outlook'. Student Tan Jun, newly returned from 'hands-on experience' in Beijing's suburbs, was quoted as saying, 'After this experience we realize we don't have a comprehensive understanding of China's socialist construction because we lack practical experience in the current reforms ... most of us don't value the current unity and stability as much as workers.' Others expressed similar sentiments, one noting that 'demonstrations and empty slogans don't do the society any good'.

The events of 1989

We [*China Daily*'s non-Chinese staff] went from being called together and told why we weren't 'playing up' the situation – two weeks ago, maybe three by now – to a quite sudden reversal in which staff reporters were actually going out and covering the news and getting it in the paper!!! At one point three-quarters of the staff was marching

in the demonstrations, with flags calling for freedom of the press and an end to corruption.
 – Letter to the authors from two American friends working at *China Daily*, dated 30 May 1989.

How times had changed in a few short years, it appeared. *China Daily* seemed to have progressed from the fearful lapdog of the party to actually taking the lead in chronicling events. But this apparent triumph of journalism wasn't the end of the story. As events unfolded, *China Daily*'s reporting took many disconcerting twists and turns that reflected the struggle within the party.

Not 'playing up' the situation
When Hu Yaobang died on 16 April 1989, *China Daily* fell in step with world media in reporting the death, the details surrounding it and the background of Hu's life. What it did not report was that anti-government protests, disguised at first in the time-honoured Chinese fashion as tributes to the fallen leader, broke out almost immediately. On the same day as it reported Hu's death, the *New York Times* reported that students at Beijing University, mourning and angry at Hu's 1987 political demise, put up illegal posters and began discussing democracy.

On 18 April, *China Daily* ran a picture of mourning teachers and students from Beijing University. A small accompanying story said that about 3,000 of the crowd visited Hu's home to pay last respects, but the story mentioned nothing of the protests that were reported in that day's *New York Times*.

The pattern of underplaying the situation was pronounced in this period. On the 19th, *China Daily* reported that 200 minority students laid a wreath at a monument to Hu; *The Times* reported that 10,000 students marched through the streets of Beijing chanting democratic slogans, and that people's opinions were being subtly expressed by smashing small bottles – the written characters for 'small bottle' resemble those of Deng's given name.

On 20 April, *China Daily* carried a small story saying that 1,000 people had tried to break into Zhongnanhai, the party leadership's compound on the edge of Tiananmen Square, but it did not say why. *The Times* reported on page 1 that more than 10,000 pro-democracy demonstrators had taken over the square, with several thousand marching to Zhongnanhai to demand a meeting with leaders.

On 24 April, the day after a memorial service for Hu that had been hastily closed to foreigners, *China Daily* carried a big story headlined 'Nation pays last tribute to late party leader Hu' on page 1, which made no reference to protests. The *New York Times* reported on the same day that a crowd, swelled to 100,000, was in the square in defiance of a ban on public protests, and that students had camped all night in the square to foil government attempts to close it to further rallies. In *China Daily*, an accompanying story reported riots and looting in the cities of Changsha and Xi'an following the nationwide public broadcast of the service for Hu, but this was treated as a strictly criminal matter with, like the lead story, no mention of political protests. A familiar pattern of coverage seemed to be reasserting itself, but this time things would be different – for a while.

'Playing up' the situation
On 26 April, *China Daily* reported on page 1 the now-famous *People's Daily* editorial of the same day calling for a firm stand against disorder (which, given the lack of mention of protests, might have seemed a bit mysterious to someone who had read only *China Daily*), and lashing out in harsh terms against those who questioned the government. This editorial sparked even larger and very angry protests, led by students who saw their sincerity being questioned and their concerns disregarded.

This turn of events led to an almost immediate change in *China Daily's* coverage. On 28 April, a page 1 story, headlined 'Dialogue proposed as students demonstrate', carried a conciliatory proposal for direct dialogue with students from an unnamed 'State Council spokesman', along with accounts of student demonstrations that stressed their peaceful nature, and mentioned that demonstrators 'also voiced support for the party's leadership'.

The coverage in early May, though at times schizophrenic and seemingly oriented towards smoothing over a still-boiling situation, was nevertheless remarkable compared with previous standards. A front-page story on 1 May reported that officials, in face-to-face dialogue with students, 'said students' wishes to promote democracy and curb corruption are completely in line with the government goal'. A page 4 opinion-piece that day included a broad range of opinions about the demonstrations, reportedly gleaned from people in the streets.

On 3 May, a report from Shanghai said that 'several thousand university and college students took to the streets yesterday afternoon', raising banners bearing such slogans as 'give us democracy and freedom'. The coverage was straightforward, detailed and largely in agreement with the *New York Times* story on the same event. The next day, in a front-page story, Zhao Ziyang urged the nation to maintain stability, and a page 1 picture showed him shaking hands with a group of smiling students. Above it, however, was another story in which the government expressed a willingness to continue dialogue with the students although rejecting an initial list of demands as 'unreasonable'. The next day, Zhao said in the paper's top story that the student demonstrations did not indicate political instability in China.

On 6 May, even the soon-to-be-reviled Li Peng became more visible. 'Li Peng puts stability as top state task' was the page 1 headline. In that story, Li said the government would strive to safeguard national stability and simultaneously to 'earnestly overcome its shortcomings and reduce corruption', adding that he was happy that students had gone back to their classrooms. Across the page, down in the right-hand corner, however, another story, headlined 'Students split over return to classroom', said that although many students had gone back to classes, some had demanded to continue the boycott.

An increasing role in the situation
On 10 May, a front-page story boldly proclaimed 'Journalists call for talks'. In it, journalists called for dialogue with the party and government officials, following promises by the authorities to conduct broad contacts 'with people from all occupations'. The story went on to say that the news

coverage of the students' activities in the past weeks was, according to the journalists, 'far from enough and not objective'.

Journalists had already marched in the demonstrations, but starting with this story they assumed an even more active role in the events swirling around them. For the brief remainder of this period of repertorial candor, calls for press freedom became an ever-louder element in accounts of demonstrators' demands. Even pictures of marchers from both *People's Daily* and *China Daily* ran during the boldest days of the coverage.

The pattern of candor continued for another ten days, with 17 and 18 May marking the boldest coverage yet. Pictures and stories sympathetic to the strikers continued on the 17th, accompanied by a page 3 picture of easily identifiable *People's Daily* reporters marching with a banner proclaiming 'press reform is a must'. A policy editorial on the opinion page spoke of the 'plight' of the students and cited the 'huge throngs' of students heading for the square. In that editorial, the paper also appealed to the party to listen to the demands of the students because 'the situation has reached a point where things are extremely complicated and could develop into social unrest or even a political crisis', adding, 'Some direct policy statement (from the government) seems necessary at this point – such as embracing their ardent wish for democratic reforms and a pledge of no retaliation in any form and at any time.' On 18 May, the paper reported that one million marchers 'from all walks of life, spontaneously demonstrated in Beijing yesterday in support of some 3,000 fasting students in Tiananmen Square.' This is indeed very bold, almost startling, for *China Daily*.

Another turn of the screw

The declaration of martial law on 20 May marked a turning of the tide, but not yet a full retreat from candid coverage. Things continued at a fever pitch on 22 May. The lead story told how the army would 'firmly carry out its orders'. An accompanying piece which was apparently placed on the front page late and without the grammatical assistance of a foreign polisher, was headlined 'Marshals say quell is rumour'. The story, which must have seemed bizarre at the time, reads in part: 'Marshals Nie Rongzhen and Xu Xiangqian denied word that the government will suppress the students with the army in Tiananmen Square last night and early morning today'. In China, a story like this can mean two things: that there is in fact a rumour, which is of course conceivable at such a time, or that just such a suppression has been discussed in high places. Other stories in the next few days reinforced the figure of one million marchers, and a story on 25 May said that foreign tourists were cancelling trips.

From 26 May, the tide of coverage turned more abruptly, and in retrospect it's easy to see why. The power struggle within the party was decided. On that day, a photograph appeared on page 1 showing 'full attendance' at the textile factory. Although sporadic stories still appeared on people from the countryside arriving to protest, *China Daily's* wings had clearly been clipped. On 28 May, the first story appeared that blamed the turmoil on 'chaos instigators'. By 31 May, the Goddess of Democracy had been erected, and a news story in *China Daily* called the statue an insult to the solemn site of national celebrations.

In early June, there was a lull in coverage until after the massacre. Stories seemed to be emphasizing that the strikers were just a nuisance. Children's Day festivities were called off. 'Helpful' soldiers at Beijing railway station were shown 'getting things back to normal'. Tourism agencies said that in their sector it was also getting back to normal, exactly the opposite of what foreign media were reporting.

On 5 June, the coverage of the massacre was restrained. 'Martial law troops are ordered to firmly restore order', read the headline. Four pages were published instead of the usual eight, a practice that continued throughout the month, and there was no other mention in the paper of chaos. Only a small notice on the front page gave a clue that things weren't normal: 'Due to special reasons, *China Daily* apologized for having only four pages today'.

What followed was, as in the 1986–7 crisis, a propaganda typhoon. There were no more protesters, only saboteurs and disturbers of public order. 'Iron fists' were urged to crush 'rail saboteurs'. On 15 June, the old appeals to learn from 'years-old-leaders' talks' arose from their

Cultural Revolution-era graves. On 17 June, exactly one month after the dramatic unsigned editorial 'Concern for strikers', which called for 'embracing [students'] ardent wish for democratic reforms and a pledge of no retaliation in any form and at any time', the same space in the temporarily smaller *China Daily* was occupied by another unsigned editorial 'Restoring order', which opened with the words: 'The Chinese authorities have recorded a major victory in putting down the anti-government riot which showed its extremely damaging nature in the first days of this month in Beijing and some other cities of this country.'

Fluctuating party policy or fluctuating control?

The political crises of 1986–7 and 1989, and *China Daily's* reaction to them as reflected in its coverage, display two different, but not completely dissimilar, examples of what can happen when the leadership of the communist party of China becomes seriously divided over policy.

It is for historians, or those with much better information on the actions and motivations of party leaders, to decide whether the demonstrations in both crises were a product of this division, whether they were an intentional stirring-up of 'the masses' to advance the cause of one faction, or a spontaneous result of the rifts becoming known, or, on the contrary, whether they were the spark that caused the disagreements. It is entirely possible that all three explanations may have been true at different points in each crisis.

Where the two crises diverged, from the standpoint of *China Daily's* coverage and actual events, was in the loss of control over events that resulted from internal party discord. This may reflect a difference in the depth of the disagreement, or in the power of individual party factions in each crisis. Again it is difficult to tell. In any event, the party was in far greater disarray at the height of the 1989 crisis than at any time during the 1986–7 crisis, a fact for which the country paid dearly, and which had a clear impact on *China Daily's* coverage.

The party's control over the news media is exercised through the Propaganda Department, which answers directly to the Central Committee. Propaganda officials, according to *China Daily* staff members, meet with media leaders regularly (usually every two weeks) to discuss news events and to deliver the party line on how they should be covered. During the 1986–7 crisis, as Hu Yaobang struggled to survive politically amid assaults on his position that the party should speed up and widen reforms – and later that it should take a relatively conciliatory line towards demonstrating students – the party line was in flux, resulting in the fluctuating coverage seen in *China Daily* and other newspapers. But for all its severity this first crisis did not throw the party into disarray. After Hu Yaobang was politically disposed of, things returned to normal rather quickly.

The 1989 crisis, however, carried with it a far more complex and compelling story. According to two *China Daily* staff members in a position to know, the disarray within the party was so complete that, at the height of the crisis – from the last week of April until some days after the declaration of martial law on 20 May – Propaganda Department officials did not hold their regular meetings with any top Beijing editors. One of these staff members said that no meeting was held from late April until after the massacre of 4 June. (As with other staff members interviewed for this chapter, the two cited here do not want their names to be used. Since these particular staff members will be quoted at some length, we shall henceforth refer to them individually as X and Y.) This lack of meetings left the editors in a difficult position indeed. Whose line were they to follow? The stakes for them personally, and for the country, could be very high, and they were all aware of it.

At *China Daily*, according to both X and Y, top editor Chen Li took a very cautious path in the absence of outside guidance.* Chen's policy was, in a nutshell, to do less than other newspapers and to do it later. If a story about student demonstrations ran in one newspaper, *China Daily* would run a shorter version the next day. A four-column picture in another newspaper would become a three- or two-column picture in *China Daily*. According to X, the newspaper did not assign its own reporters to cover the demonstrations until the end of April.

After the crisis had passed, as Y reported, it was stated at a *China Daily* editorial meeting that meetings between editors and propaganda officials

---

*The two staff members, incidentally, were interviewed separately and were not informed of the contents of the other interview until later.

stopped in April because of a rift at the very top: a disagreement between Deng Xiaoping and Zhao Ziyang over how much to restrain the press. Zhao favoured fewer restrictions. After his fall from power, the government accused him of seeking these relaxations in order to gain, through broad reporting of the turmoil, support for his position on this and other matters (like Hu in 1986, he was seeking more and speedier economic reforms, according to accounts in the world press). Y agrees with the government's assessment of Zhao's motives in this instance.

In late April, several occurrences resulted in bolder coverage at *China Daily*. Top Beijing editors met with Hu Qili, an ally of Zhao who appeared at the moment to be one of the most powerful leaders of the party Central Committee, and Hu urged them, according to X, to cover the demonstrations without restriction; the *New York Times* reported in a 29 April story that 'one of the nation's top Politburo members' told editors of nine newspapers that they could report 'the actual state of affairs' so that ordinary people could decide issues for themselves. Hu explicitly added at this meeting that there would be no press restrictions of any kind from the government for at least three days after the return of Zhao Ziyang from a state visit to North Korea (during this visit Zhao had also managed to disassociate himself from the 26 April *People's Daily* editorial that so inflamed the students). Zhao's faction appeared ascendant, says X, adding that in early May, 'we were sure the government couldn't stay on'.

Chen Li, a college friend of Hu Qili's when both were student leaders in the 1940s, was also deeply affected by an in-person visit to Tiananmen Square at this time, according to Y. And other newspapers were quick to take up Hu's offer, producing coverage that was spectacular by previous standards.

In this atmosphere, *China Daily* opened up, although Chen still stubbornly refused to blaze any journalistic trails ahead of other newspapers. During the first nineteen days of May, under fire from his own staff for what they considered to be too timid coverage (though quite daring by previous standards, as recounted earlier), and even, according to Y, under strong urging from his top three lieutenants to be more daring, Chen consistently vetoed such proposals, on several occasions ending conversation in editorial meetings by stating his wishes and then leaving the room. 'He said often during this time, "I am not an optimistic person even when signs are optimistic"', said Y. This relative conservatism, at what was nevertheless *China Daily*'s least conservative moment, may have spared the staff from harsher repercussions later.

X states that *China Daily*'s coverage was set to turn away from the daring a few days before the 20 May declaration of martial law, because Chen Li felt that the situation was out of control and had heard through contacts in the Propaganda Department that Zhao Ziyang's faction was losing its struggle. Although some prominent coverage of demonstrations continued in the week after 20 May, Y said that Chen Li 'was very generous with those stories because he could always say that Xinhua had done it first'.

From several days after 20 May, there was of course no doubt which way *China Daily*'s coverage would go. 'They [the editors] had to change their line to keep the newspaper, and because the students had lost', said X. 'Things were different now. This was another turn of the screw', said Y. Both believed that Chen Li's conservatism may have saved staff members from any serious repercussions. The opinion-page editor resigned his position, but stayed with the newspaper, and one young staff member was arrested, but not for her work at *China Daily*. No top editors were fired. Three of the top four – both X and Y say that all four had personally sympathized with the students – actually joined a government committee headed by Chen Li to 'clean up' the media. The fact that *China Daily* is not very influential domestically may also have helped, X speculates, and he adds that a casually stated good word for Chen Li from the new party leader, Jiang Zemin, at a meeting with editors after things calmed down, may also have had a bearing on the matter.

China Daily's coverage of the events of 1989 clearly demonstrates that *both* fluctuating party policy and fluctuating party control caused the repeated changes of line. For readers used to the roller-coaster nature of Chinese politics, the coverage could not have been surprising even with all its contradictions. Perhaps editions from the more candid days of coverage are tucked away in secret places where they're unlikely to be discovered until they are re-read by or shown to another generation, on another day.

Conclusion: more than journalism is at stake

The old guard's victory has proven neither hollow nor short-lived. The leaders felt that they had much to defend: a socialist system that had saved China from the perceived inequity and degradation of capitalism (not to mention the rot of Chiang Kai-shek's Kuomintang); a united China that had been so only sporadically over thousands of years; a bright-looking future; and, most of all, China's very sovereignty. Those beliefs and more are echoed time and again in basic party propaganda. They may well be taken at face value, but, even if they are only a convenient rationale, they remain the underpinning of much hard-liner policy.

Deng Xiaoping once had convinced much of the world, including the authors of this paper, that he fully understood that the reforms he was unleashing meant a diminution of communist party power. His dealings with hard-liners – including the sacrifice of his one-time heir-apparent, Hu Yaobang, in January 1987 – appeared to be efforts to buy time for the reforms so that they could take on a life of their own.

But when reforms brought calls for change with Hu's death in April 1989, the power struggle that ensued proved many observers very wrong indeed. The party, itself divided, was tragically unable to handle what was happening. This lack of a workable process for resolving conflicts leads to far worse than jangled nerves and changes of line at *China Daily*; it has been a source of conflict many times in China's past, and is partly to blame for the tragic outcome at Tiananmen. Perhaps it will one day be seen as the most important evidence of why the demonstrators' calls for a more open system were valid.

The people, including intellectuals, who are often the most vulnerable, are left by this crude conflict-resolution process to swing between hope and fear. With luck, the power struggle that often arises from political disagreement would end as it did in 1987: a leader deposed, a few 'agitators' cowed by explicit warnings, a propaganda campaign and a minimum of damage. But, in 1989, luck ran out. Until China finds a better way of settling internal differences, there is no guarantee that such cycles will not recur, to the great loss and sorrow of both China and the world.

4

Chinese newsrooms in
the aftermath of Tiananmen

KELLY HAGGART

The initial impact

On 4 June 1989, a Beijing doctor called the newsroom of Xinhua News Agency, gave his name and the name of his hospital, and said that he had two things to report. First, he had found clear evidence of amphetamines in the blood of wounded soldiers he had treated that day. The soldiers said that they had been 'inoculated' before being ordered in to clear Tiananmen Square, where, they were told, there had been a virus outbreak. Second, he thought that the injuries he was seeing among civilian casualties had been caused by dumdum bullets, which are banned by the Geneva convention on weapons that cause 'unnecessary wounding'.

The senior editors on duty vetoed reporting those stories. But the suppression of this and of other news about the massacre enraged many Xinhua journalists. For several days after 4 June almost nobody worked at Xinhua; journalists demonstrated inside the agency's compound in central Beijing. A crowd of 100 or more would gather outside the apartment block where senior editors lived, shouting out that Xinhua must tell the people the truth. Some people wanted to beat up the journalist who had been assigned to report the official version of events.

People's Daily, which normally has a midnight deadline, kept its front page open until 5 a.m. on the night of the massacre, and ran a boxed report from Tiananmen. It began: 'According to an editorial in the *Liberation Army Daily*, "a counter-revolutionary rebellion occurred last night in the capital".' Top editors were later taken to task for this use of quotation marks. The *People's Daily* item went on to say that the army had 'stormed' Tiananmen. It then listed seven Beijing hospitals that had been calling the paper constantly throughout the night with updated bulletins. The implication was that casualties had been heavy. Someone clipped out this item, put a red frame around it and posted it up outside the apartment building of the Xinhua leaders. The agency's correspondents in Santiago, Chile, sent a telex appealing to colleagues in Beijing to report the truth, and this, too, was posted up inside the compound for all to see.

An unusually large headline over a three-paragraph story in *People's Daily* on 4 June read: 'Students launch hunger strike to protest killing of students by the authorities'. The story allegedly had nothing to do with China; the dateline was South Korea. As late as 8 June, the paper was giving prominent play to foreign stories with unmistakable double meaning. On that day, an editorial picked up from North Korea was headlined: 'Condemn the fascist regime in South Korea for murdering students and civilians'.

Emotions were also running high at *China Daily*. On Sunday 4 June, the editor-in-chief stayed away, delegating responsibility for Monday's paper to the four or five journalists on shift that night. A couple of them argued that they should protest the massacre by producing a paper which contained only international news – Khomeini's death in Iran, for instance. Others argued that a more important task lay ahead than making a gesture of protest, and that was simply to survive; the English-language *China Daily* was a product of the reforms, and their best hope was to try to keep the paper going until things loosened up and an airing of views was possible again. But no one would agree to translate stories from the army daily reporting the 'victory over the counter-revolutionary students'. So they decided that the best course of action would be to wait for something to come across Xinhua's English news wire. But nothing did; the wire was silent and would be for several days.

Xinhua was in turmoil. After a few days of demonstrations, Mu Qing, the agency's director, sent a verbal message that was relayed to protesting journalists: 'Comrades, don't go too far. I share your sentiments, but I also want to try to preserve our foothold. If we don't calm down and go back to work, the same thing will happen at Xinhua as happened at *People's Daily*.' The warning did serve to calm things down.

What happened at *People's Daily* had been, as one Chinese journalist put it, 'more than a reshuffle'. The men in the two most senior posts – editor-in-chief and director – were both removed, as were almost all middle-ranking editors and department heads. Most were put under house arrest to write self-criticisms. In addition, police arrested at least two *People's Daily* reporters. The exact figures are probably not known outside the leadership, but certainly dozens of rank-and-file journalists at the paper were fired or, in other cases, suspended for a period of repentance in which to write self-criticisms. In addition, about 200 reporters and editors were restricted to working in the office, forbidden to go out to conduct interviews or cover stories.

The man in charge of the *People's Daily* foreign page was among those dismissed. He was not a radical; he was a communist of good conscience. In May 1989, he had said to the editors of the domestic pages that if they needed more space to cover the student protests they could use the foreign page. During the crackdown, he was confronted by his superiors: 'You think the newspaper is yours? It's not! It's the party's. So how can *you* give the page away?' His dismissal was a personal disaster because he was close to retirement; if he had retired while still in his post, he would have been entitled to a high pension.

Editors from the army newspaper were moved over to replace the *People's Daily* editorial board. Senior editors of provincial party papers were also brought in, people who had witnessed neither the protests nor the massacre. The party leadership evidently felt that Beijing journalists could not be trusted. It was, largely, an accurate assessment. The mood inside Beijing newsrooms was now one of simmering anger and frustration. And, with open defiance no longer an option, some Chinese journalists felt that they were badly misunderstood in the West. 'I really want to correct the impression that Beijing journalists have been supine', said one senior editor. 'In fact, the majority of us are in a rebellious mood.'

Two weeks before the massacre, when press controls were tightened again after a week of relative freedom, journalists in the capital did not submit without protest. One reason for their new confidence was that before that exhilarating week, which had extended roughly from 15 to 20

May, Party Secretary Zhao Ziyang and Propaganda Chief Hu Qili had each sent them an encouraging signal. First, Zhao gave a speech to the annual conference of the Asian Development Bank on 4 May, in which he said that the reforms would proceed and that the student protesters were well-intentioned. Then Hu Qili met journalists from *China Youth News* and other papers on 10-13 May and agreed with the general thrust of their comments on the need for press reform.

These meetings were held in response to a petition calling for talks with the government on press reform, which more than 1,000 Beijing journalists had signed. It was a case of wishful thinking, perhaps, that Beijing's newspaper editors took these cues from Zhao and Hu to mean that the moderates were winning the power struggle. In any case, the editors and their newspapers became more daring. Open, sympathetic coverage of the students stopped, however, with the imposition of martial law on 20 May. But, even after control by the Propaganda Department had tightened again, Xinhua and *People's Daily* continued to be remarkably bold, giving prominent coverage to foreign stories that contained clear allusions to the domestic situation. On 21 May, for instance, Xinhua quoted the Hungarian prime minister as saying that troops should not be used to resolve political crises, an obvious protest against martial law. *People's Daily* ran the piece on its front page.

At *China Daily,* Chief Editor Chen Li was also not happy about martial law. He told a meeting of staff who were party members: 'Probably, at this time in history, you won't have full opportunity to use your journalistic skills, but don't despair. I think this is a good time for you to concentrate on improving your journalistic skills; the time *will* come when you'll be able to use them.' Immediately after the massacre, he called another meeting, and now his tone was much tougher. He said that to those who were real enemies, the party would show no forgiveness, but that it would help those whose problems could be classified as contradictions among the people – a reappearance of the old Maoist jargon. Chen, who had liberalized coverage of the protests, now had his own survival problem.

Newsroom culture
In the ten years prior to Tiananmen, changes had begun to occur in the Chinese media. The degree of latitude available to a Chinese journalist in reporting sensitive material had come to depend on which government department controlled a particular workplace. If leaders in that department were more liberal, the paper would be likely to reflect that. The Beijing press serves as an example.

People's Daily and Xinhua are obviously the most important media workplaces, and both have the status of separate government ministries. Their directors sit on the party Central Committee and have the rank of ministers. Just below them are the two national newspapers under the direct control of the Central Committee's Propaganda Department: *Guangming Daily* and *China Daily*. These two papers have the rank of a vice-ministry, as does the State Council-controlled *Economic Daily*. Then there are the newspapers under the control of the local authorities. The *Beijing Daily* and the *Beijing Evening News* are both controlled by the Beijing municipal party committee, a bulwark of reaction. It therefore came as little surprise that, of all the Beijing papers, these two were the most conservative in reporting on the demonstrations of May and June.

There are also many other papers, controlled by various ministries, associations and branches of the party: *China Women's News*, for instance, which is controlled by the All-China Women's Federation, or *China Youth News*, controlled by the communist party Youth League. Or the *Science and Technology Daily*, which was one of the first papers in Beijing to report on the demonstrations and to give sympathetic coverage. It is controlled by the Science and Technology Commission, and its editor, Sun Changjiang, was a former ghostwriter for Hu Yaobang.

Ironically, although *People's Daily,* the most important newspaper in China, is supposed to be the party's mouthpiece, senior editors there in the 1980s were not the old-style communist editors. Before serving as party general secretary, Hu Yaobang had for a period been head of the party's Organization Department. This is an immensely powerful position that includes responsibility for important personnel decisions, including choosing senior editors for the national newspapers. With liberal Hu Yaobang placing like-minded editors in influential posts in the media, the composition of newsrooms in China began to change dramatically. The party hacks were replaced by reform-minded editors, who, although also true believers in communism, were a new breed. The party was no longer monolithic, and dissident voices were heard on the inside from people who were hopeful that the party could reform itself, that it could be pushed to become more human. Many of them had suffered in the Gang of Four period when the press was controlled by a small group of people. They wanted to guard against that ever happening again and, in general, they could see the need for a relaxation of control over the media.

Under the influence of such editors, *People's Daily*, for instance, did change significantly in the 1980s. It began carrying more human-interest stories, more objective reporting on social problems; it aired more citizens' grievances on the popular letters-to-the-editor page. It ran long, investigative pieces by its crusading reporter, Liu Binyan. Liu's exposés of corrupt local officials were extremely popular and helped inspire a genre of muckraking journalism – the *baogao wenxue* or literary reportage – that flourished in Chinese newspapers, and especially magazines, in the latter half of the 1980s.

The supporting staff at newspapers, too, began to change in the early 1980s, when newly reopened universities produced their first graduates since the Cultural Revolution. Now, for the first time, a university degree was required to become a journalist in China. Before that, two or three years' experience doing something else was all that was needed. There were few job opportunities for the new arts graduates, and journalism was a popular assignment because it was relatively interesting work. These college graduates particularly wanted to work as journalists in Beijing, to be at the centre of things. They did not want to be like the older generation of journalists, parrotting the party line. They had their own ideas; they wanted to voice their own opinions. Throughout the 1980s, professionally competent, sophisticated young people flooded into Beijing newsrooms, significantly lowering the average age and raising the educational level.

Xinhua and *People's Daily* got first pick of these graduates, snapping up the most talented and trusted. Many of them were also reform-minded. They had been seasoned by the Cultural Revolution experience of spending years in the countryside living and labouring alongside peasants; they had seen firsthand how people live at the bottom of society. They supported Deng Xiaoping's economic reforms; they also felt that changes were needed inside the media and that a relaxation of control would help China modernize.

Now in their late 30s and early 40s, this layer of people inside Beijing newsrooms wholeheartedly supported the students' calls for press freedom. But they were also experienced enough to know that if you wanted to change things in China, in places like Xinhua and *People's Daily,* you had to work gradually and from within. The best way to do that was to occupy positions of power, and by 1989 many of that generation had indeed risen to middle-ranking posts at Xinhua and all the important newspapers. When the top leadership was divided in the spring of 1989, these people were naturally inclined to side with moderates, such as Zhao Ziyang and Hu Qili.

In the final resort, however, Chinese leaders control the media by controlling the *chief* editors. Their futures, their careers, even their homes are tied to their jobs, and with the loss of position comes the loss also of all the amenities and privileges attached to it. Chief editors attend regular meetings at which they are told what they should and should not publish. They then go back to their paper and tell their deputy editors the score, and the party line is communicated on down the chain of command. In times of crisis, the Propaganda Department might well call in the chief editors on a daily basis. In between those meetings, there is always the hot line. This is the special telephone hook-up in all the most important Chinese newsrooms that goes straight to the Propaganda Department. Faced with a tricky call on a news story, a chief editor or his deputies could pick up the hot line at any time to consult the propaganda chiefs. Alternatively, they could try *not* picking up the hot line, and take their chances.

A typical case concerned the overthrow of Nicolae Ceausescu of Romania. When the news came in at *China Daily* in December 1989 that Ceausescu had been deposed, the editor on duty really wanted to run the story, so he neglected to pick up the hot line. The next day, a furious Propaganda Department demanded an explanation for the small front-page story that had appeared in the paper. *People's Daily* and Xinhua had been completely silent on Romania. Ultimately, it is the chief editor who is held responsible for this kind of gaffe. When Ceausescu's fate became clear, the news was released by all the official media because – as one *China Daily* reporter put it – 'there was no point sticking to a dead guy'.

When the Propaganda Department found it could no longer control really gutsy chief editors, the next step was to remove them and – if their liberal ideas had taken hold in the newsroom – to shut the paper down. This happened to, among others, the *World Economic Herald* in Shanghai and the *New Observer* magazine. One way around the problem of censorship had been to publish in magazines, which in China are not as tightly controlled as newspapers. In the latter half of the 1980s, with more financial resources outside state control, self-financed publications flourished. Competition among the hundreds of new titles was fierce. Advertising appeared for the first time, and editors battled to attract readers by printing material that was more daring than newspapers would attempt.

Freelancing for these magazines became a popular sideline activity for journalists. It gave them the chance to write long investigative pieces exposing the 'inside story' on things that their own newspapers would not touch. Readers soon realized that they could find in magazines the kind of things which did not appear in newspapers. Journalists themselves began to pay less attention to their day jobs and more to their freelance work. For one thing, the topics were more interesting; for another, journalism in China – although it can be relatively interesting work – is not well paid, so journalists welcomed the extra income. And freelance work could often be done on company time, because the boss in a Chinese office rarely cares very much whether staff turn up every day. Even before the massacre, the Propaganda Department had started cracking down on the small magazines, aware that they were getting out of control. Since the massacre, many hundreds more have been closed. Overall, therefore, the political culture of Chinese newsrooms prior to Tiananmen was far from monolithic.

The aftermath

In the aftermath of the massacre, a central party document was circulated to media offices instructing that one per cent of staff members were to be punished as a warning to all. People selected for punishment were to be in addition to those arrested for involvement in the protests; those were treated as separate, criminal matters. At *China Daily*, for instance, the one-per-cent rule meant that three of 300 staff members were to be served up to the government for punishment. This meant they were dismissed and also, if party members, punished by the party, most likely by expulsion.

Journalists who worked for the English-language media in China were placed in a particularly difficult position by Tiananmen. One 21-year-old *China Daily* reporter was arrested in July. Even before the protests began, her beat had been student affairs, so she was down in the square every day. And, like other bilingual *China Daily* reporters who were there, she often found herself called upon by foreign reporters or by the demonstrators themselves to interpret conversations. Those contacts with foreign journalists were later to prove very dangerous; they landed her in detention for seven weeks and cost her her job.

During the crackdown, every journalist in Beijing had to confess the extent of their involvement in the protests. The investigation began at the top, to assess the loyalty of people in the most important posts, and proceeded down through the ranks. This screening embraced the whole rank-and-file. First, the Propaganda Department circulated packages of *People's Daily* editorials and unpublished documents from the party's *neibu,* or secret file, to all chief editors. These editors were then responsible for reading the documents to their staff. Even in normal times, it is at meetings like these that the party line is communicated to Chinese newsrooms.

After that came the more intense, small-group meetings, at which everyone was required to speak out on the contents of the documents under study. These sessions are supposed to help *zhuan wanzi* – turn the subject's mind to the correct direction. They are particularly loathed, because it is here that one must speak out and lie in order to survive. The next step was the individual confession of participation in the protests. An investigation group was formed at each media workplace, and a list drawn up of all the protest activities that journalists were known to have participated in. Investigators already had a lot of names, culled from the petitions. In the heady days in May, many petitions had gone up on bulletin boards at news organizations, and, as one *China Daily* reporter put it, 'in those days we signed anything'.

At the small-group meetings, a list of, say, eighteen protest activities was read out. The group leader would ask: 'Who joined the 4 May journalists' demonstration?' A journalist would then have to confess participation and sign his or her name on the list beside that activity. And so on, down the list. All party members who had been involved also had to produce a written accounting of themselves. About 20 per cent of journalists at *China Daily* are party members; the proportion is a lot higher at more tightly controlled papers. The written self-criticism had to be accepted by top leaders at the workplace. Some young journalists had to produce three or four drafts before their self-criticisms were deemed satisfactory. On the first attempt, they often tried to remain true to themselves, to confess involvement in the movement, but to say they did it because they had hope for China, believed it could change for the better, that the party could be urged to live up to its own stated ideals and so on. These efforts were not good enough; confession to serious errors was what was required.

People often had to provide multiple copies of each self-criticism, to circulate to the various echelons of leadership. One Beijing journalist punished in the crackdown, whose father had been persecuted during the Cultural Revolution, said wryly: 'As a child, I used to watch my father laboriously copying out his self-criticisms. He had to produce several copies of each one, all written by hand. But now things are *much* better in China because we have photocopy machines, so I can make a copy of my self-criticism for whoever wants it.'

As of 20 June 1989, anyone wanting to leave China needed to extract a special certificate from their place of work confirming that they were not involved in the protests. These were difficult for young journalists to get, because almost all of them were involved. The document, which had no official name, became known as the *haoren zhengming* – the Good Guy Certificate.

In these ways the fetters on the media were put firmly back in place. Now, a news report that does not 'contribute to stability' is considered a political error. Needless to say, there is mass cynicism and frustration among journalists, with people caring even less than usual about their work. This is true not just of journalists, but of Beijing residents in general. Everyone has tales to tell of sloppiness at their workplace caused by low morale.

In the months following the massacre, top party leaders were furious about several errors at Xinhua. The most politically embarrassing occurred after a Xinhua correspondent in East Berlin heard from an East German source that Erich Honecker had been expelled from the communist party. Xinhua reported his expulsion on its news wire, even though the East Germans had not yet announced it. As it turned out, the agency was four days early with the story. Xinhua is not interested in scoops, and normally such a report – especially when it involves a good friend of China – would have been carefully checked. It was a particularly serious error for Xinhua to make because, as part of the clampdown on the media, all news about Eastern Europe was supposed to come from the agency. Even *China Daily*, which used to be allowed to run foreign wire-service stories from Eastern Europe, was now supposed to restrict itself to the news from the region as reported by Xinhua.

Another mistake that drew an angry rebuke from top leaders involved a story picked up from the Associated Press. The AP item reported that a comet had gone out of its usual orbit. At the bottom of the story, scientists were quoted as saying that chances of the comet colliding with earth were virtually nil. When the piece was rewritten by Xinhua's English service, the scientists were now high up in the story, and quoted as saying that the comet was on a collision course with Earth. News of this imminent collision caused quite a stir, not least at the Propaganda Department, where officials were keeping a close eye on Xinhua, watching for 'mistakes' that might be deliberate sabotage. There are many gatekeepers in the Xinhua newsroom, and the comet story would have been handled by several editors before going on the wire. But no one really believed these errors were intentional; instead, they were cited as carelessness caused by demoralized people whose hearts were no longer in the job.

Top party leaders suspected senior Xinhua editors of protecting younger journalists. Several months after the massacre, the central government sent in an investigation team to size up Xinhua leaders and to determine whether they were fit to stay in their posts. In particular, it was rumoured that they were after a vice-director who had headed Xinhua's Sichuan bureau while Zhao Ziyang was running the province in the 1970s. They had already removed another vice-director, who had joined two of the journalists' demonstrations in May.

The suspicion that Xinhua leaders tried to protect their people seems to have been well-founded. Xinhua has close to 6,000 employees, with about half that number working in the central Beijing office. But it appears that not one of the agency's journalists was arrested in the crackdown. One senior official said that the only arrests were of two or three men who worked in the compound but were not journalists. They had 'set fire to vehicles during the turmoil'. In contrast, at the offices of *Beijing Daily* and *Beijing Evening News* at least five members of a staff of 200 journalists were arrested.

Lessons for the future

The fate of China's media is, of course, inextricably linked to changes in the political sphere, to how things unfold in the party leaders' compound at Zhongnanhai in the next few years. The army will undoubtedly play an important role in Chinese politics in the years to come. Indeed, its presence was more apparent inside media offices in the jittery months following the massacre. On 1 January 1990, for instance, troops with machineguns moved into CCTV; Chinese leaders were not going to make Ceausescu's mistake and lose control of the central television station.

For now, the trick for journalists is to keep their heads down. One professor of journalism said that the most vital lesson he had to teach his students now was to try to avoid bravado. One student had handed in an essay with a reference to the 4 June 'massacre'. The professor called the student in and said: 'Be careful. Don't you realize all I have to do is underline that one word, hand it to school authorities and your career is over?' But the student did it again, and in another essay referred to the 'democracy movement' instead of the acceptable term, 'counter-revolutionary turmoil'. This student's defiance, the professor said, was typical of the mood in the whole class.

Despite subsequent events, the few days in May 1989 in which Beijingers got a taste of a freer press had an important, enduring impact. A senior Chinese journalist touched on this in a letter written a few weeks after the massacre:

> To me, one great consolation is that never before in Chinese history have the people felt such an acute need for a free press. Never before has it become so painfully clear to them that a free press is essential if they are to enjoy a reasonable measure of democracy.
>
> Another sign of the times is that thousands of journalists, including quite a number of senior ones, marched in support of the students and also wrote reports that were so interesting and sympathetic that people actually queued up to buy the newspapers they used to consider too dull to read.
>
> On TV as well, from about May 17 to 19, unannounced reports were broadcast live from the square. People kept their TVs on all day in order not to miss those reports. Everybody was so excited about the news itself *and* the manner of its presentation.

There is pride among Beijing journalists about those few days of press freedom. For one thing, it showed the potential of Chinese journalists. For the first time they were allowed to act like real news reporters and they did no worse at covering the story than their more experienced foreign counterparts. The students knew all along how important a free press was in order to convey their message and not have it distorted by the official media. But for almost all city people, no matter what they thought of the students and their hunger strike, that week of relative press freedom brought home to them the importance of more open, more enterprising media. Freedom of the press was no longer a complete abstraction.

Part Two

THE FOREIGN PRESS IN CHINA

5

The problem of distance

MARK BRAYNE

It is the premise of this chapter that much of the English-language Western media, including my own coverage, conveyed an inadequate picture of China during the reform years from the late 1970s until June 1989, and that this to a large extent contributed to the West's failure to foresee the tragedy of Tiananmen. This was less because of any wilful ideological bias of the kind seen during the Cultural Revolution. Rather it had to do with the difficulties of access to information within China, with contrasts between China and Eastern Europe, and with ingrained Western attitudes to China. The fickle nature of the Western media themselves, including the serious press, also played its part.

It is suggested that there were three main reasons for this, all related to the problems of distance: first, the lack of accurate and reliable source material in China itself (the distance of the correspondent from China's own reality); second, the preconceptions of editors (and public) at home about what constituted an interesting story from China – that is, the problem of physical and cultural distance; and third, linked with that, personal bias and involvement, or the lack of emotional distance.

This chapter concentrates on the problems of China coverage before the events of 1989, touching only briefly on my own experience of covering the events in Beijing in May of that year (I left Beijing five days before the army entered Tiananmen Square). The generalized conclusions drawn should not be construed as criticism of all British-based reporting of China's reform years. There were many honourable and incisive exceptions to this underlying theme.

The distance from reality: sources

To an extent probably not appreciated by even the sophisticated consumer of news in Britain, correspondents almost wherever they are rely on the local, indigenous media for most of their information. This is as true of Bonn and Washington today as it was of Moscow in the Brezhnev years, and of China in the years of reform. Sources in China even in the heyday of reforms were limited, coloured, indeed grossly unreliable. There can be few significant reporting posts where the Western correspondent is so alienated from the news story he is trying to cover. That is especially true if the correspondent has only limited Chinese, which for most of the reform years was the rule for the majority of those from British and American publications and broadcasting stations.

Available to the Western correspondent in Beijing there are Xinhua in English (the Chinese version is not available to foreigners), *China Daily*, English-language weeklies such as *Beijing Review*, the Chinese-language press and the BBC's invaluable *Summary of World Broadcasts* (*SWB*). Xinhua is strictly blinkered in its handling of Chinese news. Its task (however hard individual journalists at the agency may try to do otherwise) is to present a sanitized, ideologically acceptable picture of China for consumption mainly by the foreign media in Beijing itself. In the years between 1984 and 1987, I found Xinhua's reporting on domestic affairs inadequate, often inaccurate and always idiosyncratic. It could in no way be relied on to give a comprehensive or accurate picture of what was happening within China.

In contrast, its foreign coverage, where this did not impinge on direct Chinese interests, was at that time refreshingly unbiased, and was incomparably more readable, informative and comprehensive than, for example, the Soviet news agency TASS at that stage. This was, needless to say, less to do with high editorial investigative standards at Xinhua than a reflection of how the foreign news was put together – generally in the form of a straight lift from Reuters. Xinhua's service to foreign correspondents would, for example, be used to disseminate the latest policy pronouncements of Deng Xiaoping in his meetings with visitors from abroad. The quotations would be selective – as was easily verifiable by checking back with the visitor's party – and the purpose manipulative.

Information monitored from foreign news organizations and reprinted in *Cankao Xiaoxi* (*Reference News*), one of the main internal sources of information for the party hierarchy, had an authenticity which the local Chinese media evidently lacked.

One particularly characteristic example of Xinhua's unreliability was its coverage of the forest fires that raged through the border areas of Heilongjiang in the summer of 1987. From Xinhua, as from other Chinese media, it was impossible to work out the true picture. The correspondent heard more of heroic soldiers being shipped in to tackle the blaze than of the extent of the damage. One day the fire was about to engulf the entire border region, the next it was in retreat, and on the third day the Chinese media reported nothing. This, it might be noted, was at a time at which the media were meant to be at their most open and honest. It was never really plain whether Xinhua was guilty of dishonesty or of plain journalistic incompetence. Both were probably at work, but since in the case of the Heilongjiang fires foreign journalists were denied permission to travel north to see for themselves, there was no other information. The result was coverage that did little justice to the facts.

The same criticisms are true of *China Daily,* which, through the amplifier of Western correspondents in Beijing, became the mouthpiece during the reform years for the People's Republic. Stories in *China Daily* had an impact vastly greater than the paper's own circulation would suggest. Even so – again however hard some of its staff tried to be otherwise – it was as superficial and unreliable as the rest. Minor instances of inconsistency were legion. One edition, for example, had separate stories about bicycles in Beijing with radically different figures for the totals on pages one and three. Probably neither bore much relation to the truth, but they did satisfy the Chinese fetish about statistics, however tenuous their relation to reality.

The same was true in *China Daily*'s domestic economic reporting. Western correspondents, whose task it was to report the state of the Chinese economy, despaired of ever finding hard fact either here or in other Chinese publications. Xinhua and *China Daily* also excelled in endless soft stories about Wild Men or archaeological finds pushing further and further back the beginnings of Chinese civilization. They made cheerful reading, and about any other country would be entertaining as curiosity fillers in down-market Western papers. Yet all too often these were the items that were dictating what the outside world read about 'cuddly, appealing, but odd' China.

Chinese radio and television were important during the crisis weeks, reflecting quite clearly the power struggle under way within the leadership. In the mid-1980s, they were, for the Beijing-based correspondent, of little more than anecdotal value. There is no doubt that many of the Chinese journalists putting the programmes together would dearly have wished it otherwise, but a combination of party control and of antiquated operating practices rendered innovation all but impossible.

Radio news, for example, tended to run significantly behind the printed press – in the case of Radio Beijing's English-language broadcasts, up to 24 hours late. The main evening television news at 1900 local time was more an exercise in court reporting than a bulletin of information; it almost totally lacked hard fact and was useful as little more than a pointer to the health of the various elderly leaders as they were wheeled out to meet visitors. The live broadcast of news conferences during party gatherings was an innovation that brought brief notoriety among the Chinese viewing public to persistent Western posers of questions. But this was the nearest the Chinese broadcast media came in the mid-1980s to open reporting.

The BBC's *SWB*, published and posted from Caversham, was easily the best and most reliable source of unvarnished information as it was being conveyed to Chinese domestic consumers. This would translate radio broadcasts from both Beijing and the provinces, and it would pick up significant articles from the print media in China and in Hong Kong. However this usually arrived too late to be of much immediate news use – three days after publication in London and rather longer after many of the original articles or radio broadcasts first appeared.

In the mid-1980s, the local Chinese-language press that was available in Peking played a curiously minimal role in Western coverage, although notably in the Shanghai-based *World Economic Herald* occasional articles attracted attention once they appeared in *SWB*. During this period, information from the Chinese-language print media rarely provided enough material for specific news reports, although translations were useful for archiving. As well as scrutinizing the local media, the foreign journalist seeks also of course to generate his own information from contacts and from events of news significance, ranging from politically controversial concerts by visiting British pop groups to news conferences by Chinese officials. With neither kind was Beijing in the mid-1980s overly well provisioned.

In 1984, for example, there were weekly briefings from the Foreign Ministry, but correspondents were allowed to ask questions only once a month. This was improved the following year to two question sessions a month. Now it is questions every week, but this is still grossly inadequate. Ministries in Beijing were given nominal press spokesmen in the mid-1980s, but they remained extremely reluctant to answer questions. Even when visited personally in Beijing or in the provinces, officials were less than forthcoming with real information.

There were, of course, individual foreign journalists with good Chinese, who could both read the Chinese press and cultivate Chinese contacts, and who did not need to rely on the Chinese translators with dubious news judgment that were provided by the Diplomatic Service Bureau. But they too ran up against not only cultural barriers, preventing the transfer of authentic information out of the immediate Chinese circle, but also a breathtaking lack of understanding among most Chinese of the difference between rumour and fact.

For example, I recall discovering from one of my closest Chinese acquaintances – but not until shortly after the event – that she had been a delegate to the 1987 Communist Party Congress. In Eastern Europe in the old days, that would have guaranteed at least some insight into the political processes underway at the top. In China, nothing of the sort was forthcoming. Neither was there easy access in those years – as there had been for example in the 1970s in Moscow – to the disillusioned, Westernized few who counted themselves as dissidents.

It was easily overlooked in the outside world at the time, but the Chinese authorities for all their 'cuddly' image were not always pleasant to the Western press. In the space of less than one year in late 1986 and early 1987, three Western journalists were expelled from Beijing: John

MARK BRAYNE

Burns of the *New York Times*, for travelling by motorbike in a forbidden area; Shuitsu Henmi of *Kyodo*, for maintaining contact with Chinese news sources that was deemed too intimate and dangerous; and Lawrence MacDonald of Agence France Presse, for similar reasons. The aim was partly to intimidate the foreign correspondent, but more to frighten their Chinese contacts.

These conclusions are of course substantially generalized to illustrate the difficulties of hard news gathering in China. But the result was an awareness of what was really happening in a country that was frustratingly superficial and considerably more shallow than was the case in even the most difficult of times in Brezhnev's Soviet Union or in pre-revolutionary Eastern Europe. It might be added that the Chinese themselves, journalists included, have an only marginally more comprehensive picture of reality in their own country. There were honourable exceptions to these rules, Beijing-based correspondents with fluent Chinese who sought to delve deeper and more critically. But their probing stories also ran up against the more general problem of perception and demand outside China.

Physical and cultural distance

A Western journalist in China as anywhere else wants above all to get into print or onto the air; he or she therefore has to find subjects, and ways of presenting them, that will interest the editor. For a correspondent based in Beijing in the mid-1980s, what those editors and the public in Britain appeared to want above all was not stories about politburo reshuffles and dissidents (about whom there was almost no information anyway), but about pandas, discos, exotic new tourist destinations, wild men, body-building and pop music. The harsh reality was that other stories more closely reflecting the reality of China tended to end on the spike, or dropped off the bottom of the running order. This was not, of course, as true of the BBC World Service as it was of domestic BBC radio services. But, as with news from elsewhere in the world, Bush House was principally interested in China's various foreign dealings, rather than complex internal political developments.

China before Tiananmen was the acceptable face of communism - the mysterious Middle Kingdom embracing capitalism and trying to become like the West, the land of endless business opportunities, so completely different and more enlightened than the Evil Empire, the Soviet Union. However much one tried (and in retrospect such efforts were too often half-hearted) it was impossible to wean listeners and editors away from those pre-conceptions. So why these double standards? Why could the Chinese and not the Russians get away with such blatant human rights violations and be sure of such a positive press? There are many explanations.

China after the fall of Mao and the opening to the West was no longer perceived as a threat to the British – indeed the Western – way of life. Unlike those of the Soviet Union, China's nuclear rockets were not pointed at us. Besides which, China, even if few would say so out loud, was seen as a strange faraway land full of people who did not have the same concepts as we do of life, family values or the home. Unlike the Russians, they were not white and European.

There were those, of course, who did report China in much greater and more comprehensive detail, notably the correspondents of the Hong Kong Chinese-language press, those from Japan, and the English correspondents working for the *Far East Economic Review* and, particularly in those years, for *Asiaweek*. Willi Lam of the latter publication would compile every week, using his own sources and the leaks of Chinese insiders to the Chinese-language magazines in Hong Kong, the most fascinating accounts of infighting and factionalism within the party leadership. To the specialists it may have been gripping stuff. It was virtually impossible in my experience to get editors for domestic British radio even remotely interested in developments of this kind.

However little journalists would like to admit it, the view of Western governments compounded the problem. Working in Moscow or in the old Eastern Europe before the fall of communism, the correspondent knew that he was reporting from within a hostile ideological system, where, if any positive news were found, it would be interpreted both by him and by the listener or reader against the background of the accepted awfulness of the regime. Media perceptions and government policy fed off and reinforced one another.

In the case of China, Western government attitudes, and the interpretations being conveyed by the usual friendly diplomatic sources, were benevolent and on the reverse principle from that predominating in Eastern Europe. Therefore if unpleasant things were going on, they should not detract from the broader assessment of China's reforms as a Good Thing. Quite simply, Western Europe has always judged the Russians ultimately by the West's own standards and expected them to conform to European definitions of equality and justice. Such behaviour was not expected of the Chinese, who could safely be regarded as a curiosity. To state it at its baldest, news from China was entertainment, not information. The journalists based in Beijing had to play to those expectations if they were going to be seen to be earning their living. And, even if they did occasionally get into print or onto the air with harsher or more complicated subjects – about divisions within the leadership, for example, or the harsh handling of dissidents – these were not the stories the listener or the reader remembered. What made an impact was the From Our Own Correspondent contribution about cycling along the Great Wall and having babies in China, or the Today Programme feature about matchmaking or snooker tournaments. These were of course serious reflections of aspects of real life in China in which Westerners were justifiably interested. But they were only part of the story, and the rest, inasfar as it was reported, was all too often missed by the audience. Tiananmen, however, changed Western perceptions fundamentally and for the foreseeable future.

Emotional distance
Many Western correspondents who covered China during the ten years in question had previously worked in other parts of the communist world. In the mid-1980s, the contrast on coming to China was overwhelming. The shops in China were full, the food (on the whole) first-class, streets (at least in the warmer months) colourful, and the people in those days endlessly interested in the outside world.

In Moscow and the capitals of Eastern Europe the journalist in pre-Gorbachev days was treated by officialdom as a pariah, a class enemy, although paradoxically he had considerable access to inside information about what was going on in those societies through the dissident movements, and indeed by being able to mingle and converse reasonably unobtrusively with ordinary local people and intellectuals.

Chinese society presented the reverse problem. The cultural gulf was enormous, but officially the journalist was given the warmest of welcomes by a system that has spent centuries mastering the art of diplomatic pleasantry and of impressing the New Friend. I was not the first to fall, initially, for their charms, and freely admit that, after long years facing the ideological hostility of Eastern Europe, it took months to come down from a kind of emotional high at being in China.

China in these years was also physically opening up at a breathtaking pace that contrasted totally with the stagnation of Brezhnevite Moscow and even with the cautious early reforms of Gorbachev. Tibet, Xinjiang, the border areas with the Soviet Union; as the first Western journalists penetrated where none had gone for decades, they would find backpackers already there prising China open and bringing its people face-to-face with the outside world to a degree unparalleled at that time in the communist world.

It was difficult – no, it was impossible – not to be swept up by the enthusiasm then predominant for the whole process of reform and opening-up, and thereby lose sight of the underlying ideological nastiness of the system. Even the hardest-bitten of China-watchers joined in the euphoria, to a greater or lesser degree. In short, many journalists identified too strongly, although understandably, with what the reformers were trying to do, and they were encouraged to that end when their declared goals were contrasted with the stagnation and bloody-mindedness of other communist countries. The Western media wanted, as it were, the Good Guys to win. Too many allowed their own scepticism about the democratic credentials of Mr Deng to be overridden, and ignored the political lessons of the Chinese past, from the ferocity of power struggles at the top to the fundamental instability of the system. It is to be hoped, however, that those based in Beijing avoided on the whole the gross simplifications of some editors in the West, notably in the United States, who saw the whole reform programme as a simple restoration of capitalism. *Time Magazine*'s Beijing correspondent was deeply embarrassed when his editors named Deng Xiaoping as their Man of the Year for 1986.

Tiananmen

Because of all the above – the double standards, the earlier journalistic goodwill, the lack of reliable information – the build-up to Tiananmen failed to trigger in many people the kind of alarms that would have gone off in every journalistic mind at a far earlier stage had the same kind of trouble begun to brew anywhere in the old communist world in Eastern Europe.

This chapter does not presume to analyse the internal complexities of the Chinese power struggle of 1989 itself, or when and by whom the decision to use lethal force was finally taken, whether in the final week before the bloodshed, or much earlier, in April. But it is easier to explain the Western media's immediate failure to predict what would happen than it is to justify the West's chronic misreporting of China for the previous decade.

So what went wrong in 1989? A few superficial conclusions suggest themselves. The protests at first, although on a much larger scale, seemed to fit the pattern of student protests of the winter of 1986/7, which, however politically disruptive (as Hu Yaobang could relate), soon faded away and were easily contained. Those protests had briefly seized the West's imagination. However, once the old political status quo re-established itself and the students returned to their dormitories, the market for reports of internal political problems immediately shrank. Western editors were not interested in vague accounts of discrimination against students who had participated. And besides, by the summer of 1987, the 'Good Guys' in the shape of Zhao Ziyang appeared once again to be in the ascendant. That view had appeared to be triumphantly confirmed at the October Party Congress in 1987, when hardliners of the Deng Liqun kind seemed to have been conclusively routed. What most observers failed to take into account was the power that was still wielded out of nominal retirement by the Long Marchers, to whom the maintenance of orthodox party control was the absolute priority.

Most journalists in Beijing in May 1989 simply did not believe that the army would intervene with force. I, for example, had recently completed six weeks of filming with the People's Liberation Army (PLA), from Tibet and Yunnan to the Soviet border, and had allowed myself to be lulled about the army's willingness to obey orders to use violence; contacts within the 38th Army were saying in May that under no circumstances would they agree to be deployed against the people. The former defence minister, Zhang Aiping, interviewed for a programme on the PLA six months earlier, had been quite emotional in his denunciation of the political misuse of the army during the Cultural Revolution. There can be little doubt that these sentiments were at the time genuinely felt – and indeed Zhang and a number of other old generals were among those warning most determinedly behind the scenes in May 1989 against a repeat of that disaster.

Once the army had been halted in its tracks in Beijing by peaceful mass protest in the first midnight hours of martial law on 20 May, the coalition between ordinary people, students and, many journalists suspected, elements of the army leadership itself, seemed quite simply invincible. Euphoria took hold on all sides, bolstered by the experience of those extraordinary days leading up to martial law. The people in effect had taken control of Beijing in a mass popular uprising as the government retreated behind its walls.

The outside world now recalls primarily the bloodshed of 4 June. What was possibly of equal significance in the longer term for China was the power of the protest that preceded that violence. Journalists in Beijing in May 1989 saw a side of the Chinese people that few Westerners had observed with such intensity since before the 1949 revolution – open, caring, solicitous, generous. It was, although no one knew it at the time, a foretaste of the spirit that would be demonstrated across Eastern Europe during the revolutions against Soviet rule and communism later that year.

The political signals in the days preceding 4 June were confused. The world now knows, of course, that Zhao Ziyang was defeated politically much earlier than most observers had realised. But as the old men battled in Zhongnanhai, it was several days before Zhao's instructions to the media to open up and support the students were decisively counter-manded. In the early, ineffectual days of martial law, old-style reading-between-the-lines of several media reports suggested that Zhao was up and Li Peng down.

For example, Xinhua considerably exaggerated the size of anti-Li Peng demonstrations in Beijing; *People's Daily* and *China Daily* both contradicted Li's gloomy warnings of counter-revolutionary chaos by extolling the warmth and new-found honesty of Beijing's residents, where even pickpockets had stopped work out of respect for the students; Hungarian admonishments were reported against the use of military force against the people; and as rumours swirled that Zhao was in trouble as party leader, Xinhua said that he had in fact been invited to visit Thailand at a future date in his capacity as general-secretary, code that in normal party-speak suggested his continued political strength.

The military picture was also much clouded by statements from such respected army leaders as Marshal Xu Xiangqian and Nie Rongzhen, urging the students not to believe rumours that Li Peng was preparing to use deadly force. Although in retrospect, and recalling Deng's warnings of the need if necessary to spill blood, it seems to have been inevitable that the army would intervene, this was emphatically not the feeling in Beijing at the time.

To China watchers versed in the language of political infighting, all of this suggested that a monumental power struggle was under way, but it did not point towards violent army intervention. Looking back, it is far from certain that mistakes could have been avoided; the rules of China reporting were being rewritten by the hour, only to revert suddenly and dramatically to a much older form with the events of 3–4 June.

Conclusion
For some time afterwards, Tiananmen utterly changed Western media and public perceptions of China. Every story has been linked in some way to what happened in June 1989: 'Despite Tiananmen, life goes on' or 'after Tiananmen, things are still frightful'. However understandable, and indeed justified, this has meant that continuing important developments in China have, at least in the electronic media, for some time been under-reported, if reported at all.

THE PROBLEM OF DISTANCE

At the time of writing, in mid-1991, it does seem that the worst may be over and that reporting from China may once more settle down. It is possible that Western coverage of China will slip back before long to its apologetic, rose-tinted pre-Tiananmen form, but it may also be hoped that lessons have been learned.

6

Ideological bias in reporting China

JASPER BECKER

If a true picture of China had emerged over the past four decades, the public in the West would have been less shocked, or at least less surprised, by the Beijing massacre. The Chinese army's intervention was a surgical operation, and the ensuing campaign mild and restrained when seen in the context of forty years of communist rule. Since 1949, China has witnessed repeated political campaigns against segments of its population, from the early years of the struggle against landlords after the communists seized power, through the anti-rightist campaign of 1957, the Great Leap Forward, the horrors of the Cultural Revolution, the recent military intervention and innumerable smaller campaigns. The number of victims of persecution is not known, but in the long term it may well be shown to bear comparison with the 60 to 100 million who died under Stalin.

Although so much of the nature of the regime in China had escaped change by 1989, the Western public had generally not been presented with an image of China that matched reality. Thus, when the army crushed the student-led uprising, it created a huge emotional impact. There was strong contrast between the ruthlessness of the military intervention and the non-violent means of protest used by the students. Outsiders were taken aback by the brutality of the Chinese leadership because it shattered the accepted view of Deng Xiaoping and China.

In reality, Deng had never hidden the fact that he was running a dictatorship backed by the army and secret police. He had always made it clear that he had no time for Western democracy, or for the separation of powers between government, the judiciary and the ruling party. He openly rejected Western admonishments about human rights, especially in reference to the imprisonment of Wei Jingsheng, China's longest-serving political prisoner. It also apparently came as a shock to the Western public to discover that the Chinese people were not as happy and fulfilled as they had been led to believe. Many Westerners had come to the view that under Mao everyone at least had enough to eat, and that later under Deng there was at least more freedom than before. Many people had accepted the argument of the left in their own countries that the right to food and housing was more important than any (bourgeois) individual rights of free speech.

I had no first-hand knowledge of China before I began working there, and was surprised to discover gradually how much the reality differed from the benevolent image accepted in the West. It was equally startling to realize that part of the reason for the poor reporting had much to do with ideological conditioning. It was easy to condemn domestic reporting in China by Chinese journalists as entirely the product of the ideological imperatives of the communist party. It was something else to realize that Western reporters were guilty of the same sin, albeit in a more subtle way.

The historical context

For nearly a quarter of a century, Red China was portrayed by the US media as the land of the crazies, the human ant people, a nation bent on the domination of all Asia. That image was a mirror reflection of US foreign policy, which refused to recognize the government of Mao Zedong and prevented its entry into the United Nations.

Then Richard Nixon and Henry Kissinger decided to capitalize on the Sino-Soviet rift in the hope of using China as a strategic card in the US/Soviet power game. Nixon went to China. Virtually overnight, the American people began receiving a very different picture of China. So different, in fact, that one might have thought it pertained to a different country.

The Chinese were courteous, industrious, family-oriented, modest to the point of being shy. They had the most wonderful and ancient

LIVERPOOL JOHN MOORES UNIVERSITY
Aldham Robarts L.R.C.

cultural tradition; they were wizards of ping-pong; they loved giant pandas. In less than a year, American public opinion turned completely around. Everyone loved the so-recently hated and feared Chinese.

The author of this diatribe is, in fact, a Russian. Although Vladimir Pozner's book *Parting with Illusions* is about the US media, he could easily have been talking about the British or any other Western press.

Henry Luce, Edgar Snow, and the '1960s liberals'

The problems of reporting on China predate the communist party's seizure of power. During the 1930s and 1940s, a false impression was created of both Chiang Kai-shek's regime and the communist party. Henry Luce, publisher of *Time* and *Life*, altered the copy of his own journalists, and is largely to blame for promoting a too-favourable image of Chiang Kai-shek and his American-educated wife. In 1937, Luce made them Man and Wife of the Year. Years later, Deng was twice voted Man of the Year by *Time*, in curious repetition of what had happened before.

Although resident correspondents did their best to convey news of the corruption of the Kuomintang regime, and by comparison looked favourably on the communists, matters came to a head during the war with the dismissal of General Stilwell, as has been noted by the American historian Barbara Tuckman in *Stilwell and the American Experience*. Sterling Seagrove's book *The Soong Dynasty* also analyses how Luce and others ensured that their prejudices were conveyed to the American public, with disastrous consequences. Americans were duped into supporting a Chinese leader who was both disliked by his people and incompetent at fighting the Japanese.

After the communist victory, a lengthy and painful post mortem was carried out, and journalists numbered among those who were often unfairly blamed for the failure of American policy. The doyen of China reporters, Edgar Snow, was one of those attacked. According to him, the American media 'refused to publish any reports by eyewitnesses of the China scene except those which confirm their own wishful thinking and self-deception'. He went on to warn: 'The danger is that Americans imagine that the Chinese are giving up communism – and Mao's world view – to become nice agrarian democrats. A more realistic world is indeed in sight. But popular illusions that it will consist of a mix of ideologies, or an end to China's faith in revolutionary means, could only serve to deepen the abyss again when disillusionment occurs.' After 1979, much Western reporting did serve precisely to create a new image of 'nice agrarian democrats'.

In the event, Snow was both criticized by right-wing Americans for his book *Red Star over China*, being condemned as a fellow-traveller who romanticized the communists, and repudiated by the left-wing Americans. In recent years his book has been published in Chinese by the communist party in order to re-educate its members about their own party's history. The significant point is that Snow's reporting was, one way or the other, assumed to have had an ideological bias and was undoubtedly used for ideological reasons. Whatever his prejudices, Snow seems to have carefully recorded what he saw and what he thought about it, which is about all anyone can expect of a good journalist.

China reporting subsequently became, as Pozner has observed, a significant battleground in the wider struggle by the United States to oppose the expansion of communism. The cold war was actually, after all, fought in Asia. The left in the West promptly transferred the hopes it had misplaced in Stalin's Soviet Union to China. Although Mao faithfully duplicated all Stalin's policies – collectivization, the suppression of minorities, the persecution of the intelligentsia – and created an atmosphere of considerable terror, an extraordinary procession of 'liberals' came to China on 'guided' tours to return to the West with glowing reports. Characteristic of the books written in this vein is Kurt Mendelssohn's *In China Now*, published in 1969. A Berlin-born Oxford physicist, he travelled around China during the Cultural Revolution. Mendelssohn found the cult of Mao quite sane and reasonable, and saw no evidence of civil strife or any violence. He rejects any suggestion of ideological bias, claiming only to have a deep respect for China's culture.

American journalists (except for Snow) were not permitted to enter China at this time, and there were few Westerners resident there. Truthful

LIVERPOOL JOHN MOORES UNIVERSITY
LEARNING SERVICES

reporting of events in China was easily dismissed as propaganda by those who viewed it in the context of the cold war and the Vietnam conflict. Mendelssohn and similar writers left a far greater impression on a generation convinced that in China there was an earnest and honourable attempt to create a form of socialism especially relevant to the Third World. A whole generation in the West grew up accepting this view.

The official view

From 1979 a new dimension was added. Increasingly Deng Xiaoping became popular with the American right for exposing the horrors of Mao's China, for his pro-capitalist rural reforms and for a foreign policy helpful to Western interests. This was carried through to official policy during the presidency of Ronald Reagan. Although the suppression of the Democracy Wall movement and like protests were well reported in the West, the overriding impression was that the Chinese were moving steadily towards capitalism and a respect for human rights. When Reagan visited in 1984, he spoke of 'so-called communist China'. Margaret Thatcher wanted to see in China evidence that market forces could transform a Stalinist economic system; indeed, there was plenty of evidence that rural reforms had dramatically boosted food output.

The British government had a further interest in promoting a positive image of Deng's China: the Hong Kong agreement. Clearly, it would be unacceptable to hand over Hong Kong, or indeed negotiate any agreement, if Deng was running a shaky and corrupt dictatorship that survived because its citizens were exhausted and intimidated by events of preceding years. The British embassy and the government were always keen to discourage negative reporting on China. Briefings were always upbeat and optimistic. To allow them to be otherwise would undermine confidence in the Hong Kong agreement.

In private, embassy officials might dissent, and there may well have been arguments within the FCO. The more transparent American system of government occasionally afforded insights, since startling differences sometimes existed between the reports from Hong Kong-based diplomats and from those in Peking. The former were far more negative. There were other issues, such as Cambodia, over which the West needed

China's help. And the promise of huge new markets in China tended to discourage negative reporting. All this contributed towards fostering the view that China was stable and that the Chinese government was popular. The legitimacy of the regime could not be questioned. Whereas reports on South Korea consistently referred to its government as a military junta which had seized power in a bloody coup, it was impossible or rather inconceivable to refer to Deng's government in the same way. He could not be termed 'ex-general Deng Xiaoping' who seized power in a military-backed coup in 1976.

The fact that there had never been elections in China, and that the party was responsible for crimes against its own people, was not discussed. Instead, visiting politicians expressed admiration for the way that Chinese leaders controlled such a vast country, without looking closely at how it was done. Similarly, experts from the World Bank observed with enthusiasm that China was wonderful to work in, especially compared with India, because orders were given and obeyed.

Bias in reporting China
The journalist's dilemma

But if official attitudes toward China were almost uniformly positive, surely journalists at least were free to write what they pleased? This is only partly true. Of course, we were not like Chinese journalists, who are issued strict instructions on the subject and content of their articles. Nobody told us what to write. Editorial decisions are not made in Whitehall or in the Embassy. Yet journalists must reflect the prevailing political concerns of the time. They react to what politicians are saying. If visiting politicians are not prepared to comment on the authoritarian nature of Chinese leaders, there is no incentive to either prove or disprove what those leaders are saying. For example, rarely did visiting congressmen or other leaders request permission from the Chinese government to visit prisons.

In one way at least, the Chinese political scene was unique. Most dictatorships have an active opposition either inside or outside the country. Unlike in Poland, Hungary, Czechoslovakia, the USSR, Cambodia, East Germany, or even Bulgaria and Romania, there was for a long time simply no one in China to talk to who could present a case against the Chinese government. No one could be contacted who had been detained, no one who would issue a statement.

It was impossible to gauge what Chinese people really thought about the party beyond guessing on the basis of talks with Chinese friends. It was thought too risky to quote them. It was easy then for the rest of the world to assume that the vast majority of the Chinese supported the government, that it was in effect a country without major dissension or conflict. Of course there were protests in 1976, 1979 and 1987, but these were not sufficient to keep a running story going. However, in the case of right-wing dictatorships supported by Western governments, there was always a very vocal opposition backed by the left, perhaps funded by Moscow or Libya. But in any case with genuine grievances.

The left in neither Britain nor France were interested in criticizing China, to which they had given so much support. It was still a socialist and Third World country. The left, who had applauded Mao's 'experiments' in socialism, had no incentive now to report on the true nature of the current regime, since it made their past assessments look even more foolish.

My articles on the aftermath of the Cultural Revolution were printed in my newspaper with some reluctance. Six months before the Tiananmen movement started, a series of articles, describing the true situation in China, was spiked. 'What would people say if they read this?' was my editor's comment. The features editor simply said that, as far as he was concerned, nothing of interest had happened in China since the start of the reforms. The situation was similar at *Le Monde*.

The main criticisms of those who knew anything about China were about the agricultural reforms, showing that they were not working as well as the party claimed. The opinions of those who defended past rural policies (such as William Hinton, author of *Fanshen*), or the policies in Tibet, were given unusual prominence. China's support of the Khmer Rouge during these years received absolutely no censure in the numerous articles written on the country by writers who were anxious to highlight only the role of the British or American governments in Cambodia. It therefore escaped the awareness of most people that the Chinese had armed and backed the Khmer Rouge throughout its unpleasant history. China was unique in being a dictatorship that received less than its fair share of criticism, whether from the right or from the left.

The Chinese government for its part was adept at hosting foreign visitors with the banquet routine and a good deal of flattery. Western politicians went out of their way to pay homage to China's great culture and history. Well-known journalists, experts and sinophiles of all kinds were wary of crossing their Chinese hosts and jeopardizing their access to top leaders. It was not possible, after all, to be a successful China expert if you were no longer welcome in China. The charge against such people must surely be that they transferred their sympathy for the Chinese people to their masters by confusing the two.

Practicalities and preferences

But what, in practice, could Western journalists have done to highlight the nature of the regime? This question is far harder to answer. It was almost impossible to penetrate the secrecy surrounding important issues. It was simply very hard to find out anything that the Chinese did not want disclosed. Interpreters were under strict instructions to reveal nothing other than what was in the press. Real news about daily life was not usually released in the press, but passed on in meetings at work units. If the price of winter cabbage was going up, it would not be announced in the press.

There are very few ways of bypassing the authorities because so little information is available to any Chinese except those in the top levels of the party. Instead, there are only rumours. It is astonishing that in 1989, when dissidents composed a letter to Deng petitioning for an amnesty for political prisoners, they found it hard to draw up a list of names. They had in desperation to resort to reports by Amnesty International.

Chinese youth know very little about the recent past because their parents have often been reluctant to tell them. In such a situation, it is hard to find out what is going in Peking, quite apart from the rest of the country. Even if people did know, they were reluctant to talk to journalists. Contact was severely restricted. It was still normal even in the late 1980s for Chinese to report the visits of foreigners to the police.

The attitude of editors back home did not encourage a great deal of enterprise in this direction. China was not a place for investigative journalism in the normal sense. They knew what the story was: pragmatism (Deng's comment 'it does not matter what colour a cat is as long as it catches mice' was repeated in nearly every article) and the problems of getting rich. There was not much of a market for stories that bucked this trend.

Leading American journalists known to me complained angrily about the reluctance of their editors to run stories about the real nature of life in China. Nobody wanted to hear about oppression at that time. Furthermore, the problems of reforming the Stalinist economic system were complicated, and it was hard to make sense of them unless the reader fully understood how such economies were run in the first place. In the end, the correspondent was left with reporting what the Chinese themselves reported. If the Chinese press was full of stories about the role of factory managers versus that of party secretaries, then that was what the Western journalists wrote about. There was no point in writing about prisons if access was impossible, when entry could be obtained, for example, to factories.

Anyone who did fight against this tendency often got into trouble. One example concerned an article by Galen Rowell, an American wildlife photo-journalist, called 'The Agony of Tibet', which eventually saw the light of day in the Greenpeace magazine of March 1990. In it he explained how his articles went unpublished in the United States for fear of Chinese retribution. Rowell describes how he paid numerous visits to Tibet to photograph the local wildlife, only to discover that the forest and herds of wild animals that had once existed had disappeared. They had simply been wiped out by the Chinese in what he termed an environmental holocaust. When he first discovered the extent of the disaster, he gave one of America's leading news agencies the story. A correspondent in the United States then told him that they could not afford to print it because it would put their Beijing bureau in jeopardy.

Rowell claims that many US magazines were unwilling to criticize China for fear of being punished by a denial of future access, and his reports went unpublished. Editors told him that readers wanted up-beat stories, and that, after all, 'China is our friend'. A major publication did want to report his discovery, but in the end produced a straight ethnographic story leaving out all but a paragraph mentioning the lack of wildlife and forests. Even so, this prompted the Chinese embassy immediately to issue a public complaint. Rowell claims he was tried and sentenced in absentia by the Chinese for sedition. 'I began to see how the Chinese could censor the US press almost as successfully as their own', he said.

The other problem was simply the ingrained prejudice of editors at home. They often regarded China as an oriental society with an ancient civilization, and expected its inhabitants to be quaint and curious. Stories which reflected this went down well. It is striking how the same kind of stories were also well received during the 1930s and 1940s. In *China Reporting*, a survey of American journalism during that period, stories about eggs which could stand on their small end did well. In my case, it was a story on a new technique of penis transplant.

Conclusion

To see China only as a repository of the weird and wonderful, as we have always done, betrays serious ignorance and not just a concern with triviality. The key to understanding China must be to realize that it has much in common with the former Soviet Union and the East European nations now in process of transformation. It is indeed relevant to raise the issues of reform and freedom as they have been raised in Eastern Europe and the USSR. Instead there has been a general acceptance that oriental despotism has been okay in the Orient, part of the natural order of things, in spite of the fact that practices common in China would cause storms of outrage in South Africa. Chinese rulers have not been expected to behave as well as white rulers. In my view, it is time the idea that 'life is cheap in the East', with all its condescension, was set aside once and for all.

7

Accuracy and chaos: reporting Tiananmen

JOHN GITTINGS

The road to Tiananmen

It was war or very close to it in Beijing on the night of 3–4 June, and for the next weeks the city was under wartime occupation. But very few of the journalists covering the Chinese democracy movement had any experience of being under fire. Many were China specialists, either permanently based or rushed out two weeks earlier when martial law was declared. Others were diplomatic correspondents who had arrived with Gorbachev and stayed on. Nearly all had caught the contagious enthusiasm of the students, who believed – had to believe to sustain their courage – that the communist party's conservative elders would back away from military confrontation. Anyone with doubts needed only to walk to the nearest street corner and consult the citizens of Beijing who manned their makeshift barricades. 'Of course the army will never dare to come in', the cheerful workers, men and women from Beijing's network of residential 'hutongs' or lanes, told anyone who wanted to listen. 'We'll persuade them to go away.' Having checked the army on its first rather chaotic attempt to move in during the weekend of 20–21 May, they were confident of doing it again. (Hardly anyone realized that the operation had in all probability not been intended to succeed.)

In easy but essential retrospect, the foreign journalists failed to understand either that night or in the next tense days that they were watching a military operation, which was never very well organized. The army shot deliberately to get people out of its way, although some units found excuses for not doing so on the basis of purposely imprecise orders

84

from above. The soldiers killed about a thousand people, most of them non-student citizens of Beijing who sought to bar their way with remarkable and mostly unarmed heroism. Body counts are notoriously hard, as we know from Vietnam and Bucharest. The army did not kill several thousands, nor did it actually mow down hundreds in the square itself or burn their bodies. These subsequent rumours distracted the journalists from extrapolating a more accurate figure from the numbers seen in hospitals, though the reality was bad enough.

Several months later, a Chinese friend with long military experience listened to a detailed account of what I had seen on the night of 3–4 June and on subsequent days up to the 7th. That was the notorious occasion when troops marching out of Tiananmen Square – supposedly leaving in peace – shot wildly around the International Hotel one mile east of the square and in the nearby diplomatic quarter. The incident led to an official US protest and panic evacuation of most foreigners from Beijing, although in reality the atmosphere calmed immediately afterwards. 'Out of control', the friend responded. 'They were simply out of control.' Young provincial soldiers – the Beijing citizens called it a bumpkin army – were in a state of alternate panic and bravado. Their officers failed to control them largely because they in turn received no proper directions from above. It has also become clear that the top leadership deliberately avoided giving explicit instructions to the army in the field. Thus, no one could be clearly labelled with responsibility except the troops, including those who did not fire a shot and later deeply resented their enforced complicity. But at the time there was a general assumption that every event which was witnessed formed part of a coherent plan.

The massacre and its aftermath also largely swept away the memory of the Western media's collective misjudgment in concluding that it could not happen. A few days before, it had been suggested in a conversation among British journalists that Li Peng might engineer a provocation to force the issue, staging some incident in the suburbs in which three or four civilians might get killed. This was regarded as a far-fetched hypothesis, and the consensus was that such an incident would provoke a city-wide rising against him.

The journalists were fooled again just one night before the massacre, when there was a ludicrously botched incursion. Young unarmed soldiers jogged 20 kilometres into the city centre. Others in civilian clothing, but wearing army trousers, tried to infiltrate individually. They were all spotted, turned around, roughed-up a bit or just told off by the Beijing mums, and sent packing. After a second failure, the media representatives argued (the army had already been checked two weeks before when martial law was declared), surely it would refuse to be humiliated a third time.

Strangely enough it was possible to form a clearer perception of the risks being run by the democracy movement when one was not so near to the scene. On the spot, the mood was so exhilarating that most colleagues had no time or patience for the boring China-Watching chores of reading between the lines in the official press. This kind of textual analysis had in any case become unfashionable among China specialists and journalists during the 1980s, when the greater opportunities to travel and talk with real Chinese were so much more rewarding. Yet a daily reading of official messages of loyalty in the two weeks before the massacre would have shown that the reluctant army was being brought inexorably into line. To be fair, confusion was also caused because a section of the media, having broken away from central control, continued to print its own optimistic assessment of the popular movement. But it should have been seen more clearly that in many cases the dissenting media were simply recycling speculative stories from Hong Kong, which were then dispatched back to Hong Kong by the journalists.

The nature of the power struggle at the centre was also imperfectly understood, not only by the journalists but also by the great majority of student demonstrators. Optimism should have been dispelled when the moderate communist party secretary-general, Zhao Ziyang, was ousted just before martial law was declared. Instead it was widely believed that the victors in the struggle, Premier Li Peng and President Yang Shangkun, could somehow be evicted by an obscure constitutional process involving the National People's Congress. This was defective logic. The students were demonstrating in order to bring about a constitutionality which did not yet exist. It could hardly materialize now to save them. The error was compounded just days before the massacre, when hundreds of thousands marched to the single slogan of 'Down with Li Peng'. He had already won.

In longer historical retrospect, the escalation of conflict is awesomely obvious. It dates back to the beginning of 1989 when dissenting scholars joined together in a petition for a political amnesty. The chronological coincidence of two forthcoming anniversaries – the 70th anniversary of the birth of China's first democracy movement (4 May 1919) and the 40th anniversary of the People's Republic (1 October 1949) – was anticipated on both sides. But the unexpected event of the death of the former and relatively liberal party leader, Hu Yaobang (victim of the last conservative reaction in 1987), brought the students onto the streets. For the first time since the communist party took power, scholars and students joined together to demand political reform. Already the party elders were warning, not too subtly, that if their rule was threatened they would use any means to defend it. They were already demanding the resignation of Hu Yaobang's successor, party Secretary-General Zhao Ziyang. Deng Xiaoping had already dismissed the importance of world public opinion if the authorities were forced to take action. In Tibet, martial law had already been declared after the army shot demonstrators early in March.

Yet because the leadership was divided, the first demonstrations in Beijing were allowed to gather momentum. The students escalated their challenge from denouncing official corruption and nepotism to probing the feudal origins and characteristics of communist party rule. When half a million took to the streets on 27 April, and again on 4 May, sweeping aside token lines of police, the movement seemed to assume the shape of China's legendary Monkey King, invincible with his Golden Staff which cleared the heavens of dust. The China specialists were excited by the sight of a successful mass movement; the diplomatic correspondents were amazed by the sight of Mr Gorbachev being ushered by the back door into the Great Hall of the People. Most did not pause to think that tanks can be stopped by people lying down only if the commander has already been ordered not to keep going. One individual, it is true, may sometimes stop one tank, as did happen once *after* the massacre. But it was an isolated incident in full daylight.

The two armoured personnel carriers (APCs) that swept along the

Avenue of Everlasting Peace around midnight on the 3rd kept going. With thousands of other Beijingers, a few foreign journalists ran after one of them but could not keep up. At the first set of barricades, the citizens voiced their indignation that it had crushed a few bicycles. That already seemed an enormous crime. On entering the square, it crushed people. One of the APCs, perhaps this one, was stopped by poles pushed into its tracks. The crew of five was dragged out and at least two were lynched – by Beijingers; the students tried to save their lives. In less than an hour the democracy movement was engulfed in blood. Further west along the avenue, dozens, perhaps hundreds, of protesters were being shot down.

The media respond

Most of the Beijing-based foreign journalists with transport and good information had already headed west towards the Nationalities Hotel and Muxidi and seen the slaughter there. Others followed the crowds that reformed after each episode of violence and drifted almost involuntarily towards the square. They approached from the east, along the avenue which divides the top of the square from the Forbidden City. When the tanks and the troop carriers arrived from the west, they slowly but systematically secured the northern perimeter by shooting at intervals into the crowd. Most of the watching journalists retreated east towards the Beijing Hotel. A very few journalists – perhaps half a dozen of all nationalities – moved south towards the centre of the square where thousands of students waited around the Martyrs' Memorial.

This is why there does not exist a fully comprehensive account of events in the square between 2.30 and 6 a.m., by which time most of the students had been allowed to retreat through the southwest corner. Within hours it was being reported that hundreds, probably thousands, had been mowed down by machine-gun fire, or crushed in their bivouac tents by tanks. This did not happen, although a small number of students and workers may have stood their ground and invited death, either in the open or (less probably) by remaining deliberately in their tents. The authorities tried to avoid killing students, just as they made no effort to avoid killing Beijing civilians. (After all, the students despite their opposition were still 'intellectuals', many with parents or relations in the government bureaucracy.) But, once the students had left the square, they were as vulnerable as anyone else. At least eleven were crushed by speeding APCs as they crossed the avenue northwards just a mile to the west, at the Liubukou junction.

It is now clear that the journalists did not understand either that night or in the next tense days that they were watching a military operation. The army shot deliberately to get people out of their way to 'clear the road' (*kai lu*). According to the best estimates, they killed well over a thousand people, most of them non-student citizens of Beijing who protested with remarkable heroism. Dozens were seen on Western television, filmed by cameras from balconies of the Beijing Hotel, being mowed down on the morning of the 4th as they attempted to approach the army lines and remonstrate. The army also shot innocent people because individual soldiers panicked or were just hyped up (the not-very-likely rumour had it that they had been drugged). Its convoys headed east and west on what seemed to be inexplicable missions. The rumour rapidly spread that they were manoeuvring to deter punishment from other 'good' army units, which disapproved of the slaughter.

On the morning of the 7th, from a room in the International Hotel, I watched soldiers of the 'good' 38th army shooting at a crowd of spectators just below. Three hours later, units of the 'bad' 27th army were observed withdrawing to the applause of the same crowd. Without warning they then shot exuberantly in the air for at least ten minutes, peppering the hotel with bullets. Half a mile further east they shot at windows in the diplomatic quarter. The Americans later protested at this 'deliberate' act of violence, although it could just have been craziness. The Hong Kong press, however, subsequently reported that army units had deliberately been mixed together from the start to avoid correct identification.

Many foreign journalists, including myself, were in China on tourist visas – a practice that had caused no problems in the past. There was some nervousness now. The International Hotel closed down and it was necessary to move to the Palace Hotel, which was away from the shooting and part-owned by the People's Liberation Army. The argument was that the army would not shoot up its own investment. No one came to check the visas. A few journalists – mostly high-profile film crews – got into trouble if they were picked up while filming. Otherwise the usual security services had stopped operating once the army moved. There were no checks of any kind at the airport, even two weeks later.

Accuracy and chaos
Was it a massacre?

What happened exactly? How much violence was there against the army, and should that affect one's moral judgment at all? Was it a massacre or a large-scale military operation that killed a lot of people? Do these questions matter in the light of the basic truth that the Chinese government had declared war on its own people (the *Guardian*'s headline on 5 June, which in retrospect remains the right one). The body of journalists did well in circumstances under which most were extremely unfamiliar. But there was a lot they did not understand, and some felt an awkwardness not solely attributable to modesty when they were congratulated on returning home.

A massacre is 'a general slaughter usually of unresisting persons', and therein lies its peculiar horror. But it takes two things to inscribe a massacre on the pages of history: the actual commission of the event, and the widespread dissemination of news about it. The Beijing massacre was particularly well reported, and formed the first example of a category of highly visible upheavals on the international scene in 1989–90. Satellite telephones and dishes, video cameras and rapid transmission, worldwide dissemination of news, particularly by the Cable News Network (CNN), all played their part. The image of students and tanks is one of those framed in CNN's self-advertising film, along with the Romanian revolution and the Soviet coup. Indeed, the very term massacre soon acquired a family of cognate examples: Beijing, Bucharest/ Timisoara, Baku, Tbilisi and Vilnius.

But was it after all a massacre? It was certainly not the 'Tiananmen massacre' as popularly imagined. The location may still be close enough to the actual scene where many died; they fell on Changanjie, the Avenue of Eternal Peace, which was only technically distinct from the northern side of the square. Yet it was not a 'general slaughter' of the people in the square, although this is how it is usually remembered. Nor was it, for the reasons given earlier, a general slaughter at all. The army had its orders to proceed to the square and to overcome any obstacles on the way. Perhaps those responsible secretly hoped that the people of Beijing who had been blockading the streets for the past two weeks would be 'taught a lesson'. On the other hand, since many of the barricades had come down, they may have hoped to secure the square with very little bloodshed. If at any rate it was a massacre, it was the 'Beijing massacre' – a description that also pays tribute to the ordinary people of Beijing who bore the brunt of the killings.

Most massacres are essentially political acts, but usually also mobilize popular hatreds and fears to serve their purpose. The Beijing massacre was a wholly political act, relying on no hatred or fear except that experienced by young out-of-town soldiers who had been warned that desperate class enemies were ready to take their lives. It was massacre as an act of state, and justified afterwards on those grounds.

Partisan reporting

The manner of reporting massacres is also bound to be partisan and politicized. One account, favourable to the official forces that have in most cases promoted the massacre, will stress the violent and menacing behaviour of the 'mob', requiring the use of armed force to suppress it. Another account, sympathetic to the victims of the massacre, may exaggerate casualties and atrocities. Both types of account became available soon after the events of the first week of June 1989.

The versions of student eyewitnesses (although several of these relied on secondhand evidence for the final crucial hours in the square) were written in a style of protestation and denunciation which can be traced all the way back to the student manifestos denouncing government terror in the 1920s and 1930s. The same hyperbolic style also appeared in the Cultural Revolution, when rival factions alleged 'bloody massacres' had been committed by their enemies. Although these accounts contain some accurate information, they need to be carefully sifted. The most useful are not those written by named leaders of the student movement, but those by anonymous participants, who bring out the random and haphazard nature of the violence as well as the spontaneous bravery of those who stayed on to defy the army.

Official Chinese publications have made the most of the violence committed by young Beijing resisters against the army, some (but not all) of which undoubtedly provoked individual soldiers or units to respond lethally. It is hard to establish a proper sequence for these events, and there are suspicions that the Chinese authorities tampered with their own video evidence so that violent popular responses to the army's use of fire were presented as provocation. Nevertheless, the Chinese sources do contain a reasonable amount of detail that could usefully be collated. There are also internal inconsistencies that reveal the weakest areas in the official case – for example, avoidance of any mention of the daylight killings on the 4th and the 7th that were widely witnessed. It is of course possible that some of the official accounts, which reproduce extensively the claims of those protesting the massacre – in order, it is said, to rebut them – have been written with an ambiguous purpose. Even the English title of the most accessible official account can be read two ways: *Beijing Turmoil: More than Meets the Eye* (Che Muqi, Foreign Languages Press, 1990).

Both Amnesty International and Asiawatch issued quite detailed accounts. Amnesty's 'China: The Massacre of June 1989 and its Aftermath' (April 1990) contains several eyewitness accounts and is reasonably comprehensive but not always accurate, being based on a provisional document which Amnesty issued very soon after the event in August. It repeats the quite inaccurate claim that 'at least 300 people' were killed on 5 June in Chengdu, capital of Sichuan province. It also records without critical comment the unsubstantiated claim that up to 200 civilians remained in the square after it was cleared and that they were 'reportedly executed summarily five days later'. Asiawatch published a very full dossier compiled by its researcher Robin Munro, one of the very few foreign observers who risked their lives by remaining in the square. Asiawatch's brief formulation of the events is also the most accurate: 'Several hundred', it says, 'and perhaps as many as a thousand of these "counter-revolutionaries" were killed on the streets of Beijing by the Chinese army as it converged from all directions on Tiananmen Square on the night of June 3–4' (*Punishment Season: Human Rights in China After Martial Law*, February 1990).

4 June in retrospect

Time moves on, and the rush of changes on the international scene quickly obscures the past. What happened in Beijing was not unfamiliar; the armed wing of the state apparatus of many countries has used firepower to intimidate and suppress popular movements many times in the past, and will do so again. Some such incidents receive more attention than others. The Indonesian massacre of 1966 remains almost entirely unresearched, although it caused the death of probably 200 times more civilians than in Beijing. However, the army massacre on East Timor in November 1991, witnessed by foreign journalists at a time when some international attention had focused on Indonesia's occupation of this territory, caused a relatively much greater stir. Whatever the details of what happened in Beijing, it is a massive blot on the reputation of the government that authorized it or allowed it to happen, and a scar on the consciences of many of those involved. Eventually we may expect that a new regime will disinter the evidence and label those who were guilty – although perhaps, as in the case of the Gang of Four, this will involve some degree of historical distortion. Journalists in the meantime can and should learn from the experience. Individually they may not find themselves in a similar position again. Collectively, whether on the spot or at the news desk, or in opinion columns and editorials, many journalists will face similar hard questions of fact and judgment.

8

Television and Tiananmen

ROGER SMITH

Just after midnight on Sunday 4 June, the tension in Beijing was shattered by the unmistakable sounds of assault – the rumble of an armoured personnel carrier (APC), answered by screams of protest and panic from the crowd in its path.

After a night on the lookout around Tiananmen Square, we have stopped at the Jianguomenwai overpass, about a mile to the east along Changan Avenue. A crowd of several thousand has disabled a military convoy and pushed several truckloads of frightened soldiers into the road as an obstacle to any assault. We do not know that, several miles to the west, tanks and troops are already fighting their way towards the square. For foreign camera crews, as for the Chinese around us, it is a guessing game. From which direction would assault come? Would it come at all? Our questions are suddenly answered by the APC speeding towards us. It breaks through the fleeing crowd and, as our camera hones in, pivots two hundred yards down the road and roars back towards the roadblock. Without slowing, it crashes over one of the trucks, spilling soldiers into the crowd behind.

A moment of silent shock gives way to a rising chorus of outrage. We rush towards the truck. As if by magic, the crowds part at the sight of our camera; this is what they want the world to see. In a pile of crumpled bicycles lies at least one body, head crushed beyond recognition in a spreading crimson stain. Our camera zooms in for a sickening close-up. These are among the first pictures of one of the victims of the assault on Tiananmen Square. But it will be almost 24 hours before our viewers in

94

Canada will see them; the Chinese authorities have pulled the plug on satellite transmissions for television. It is a naive and futile tactic, resulting from the outdated belief that they could completely control the media and hence the image portrayed of China abroad. Within hours, the first videotapes will be smuggled out of China and transmitted for a waiting world to see.

Reporting for television

My impressions of how television performs in China spring mainly from my experiences working as correspondent for the Canadian Television network (CTV). I was posted in Beijing from mid-1985 to mid-1987. Those were days when economic reform topped the agenda, when officials promoted the line that 'to get rich is glorious' and optimists hoped that political reform might follow. When I left in 1987 a campaign against 'bourgeois liberalization' put those hopes in doubt, and I returned in late May of 1989 to see them crushed.

The biggest roadblocks to thoughtful television coverage of China, as with all media coverage, are xenophobia, secrecy and bureaucracy. If television is the irresistible force, then Chinese officialdom is the immovable object. If they do not want a story done, it is next to impossible to do it. Television, goes the old cliché, is the thousand-pound pencil. It requires pictures and sound; it cannot easily run stories, like print can, based on 'unnamed sources' and 'Western diplomats'. It is big and awkward and obvious; it can rarely sneak into restricted areas without being spotted.

The needs and limitations of television play into the Chinese belief that the media, and the image of China that they send abroad, can be controlled and manipulated. To film almost anything, and to travel to many parts of the country, official permission is required. No problem if you want to film a story on the abundant watermelon harvest; big problem if you try to do a story on prison labour. 'No' is the safest answer, especially in times of political uncertainty; 'It is not convenient' rings in the ears of every correspondent.

The secrecy and bureaucracy are reinforced by technical barriers and censorship. In the past, for example, natural disasters like floods often went unreported on Chinese television, and reporters were barred from travelling to affected areas. News of political disturbances is similarly censored. Even when correspondents do manage to obtain pictures, the Chinese can still restrict the means to deliver them. During student demonstrations in Shanghai in late 1986, there were long delays and high-level meetings before authorities finally granted permission to use satellite equipment. In 1987, my successor obtained some of the first pictures of the aftermath of uprisings in Tibet. He had to fly all the way to Tokyo in order to transmit the material to Canada. Even now, stories are monitored by censors at the CCTV satellite centre; sensitive material can be struck out, although sympathetic technicians will sometimes diplomatically turn an eye. Covering sensitive stories is much easier for print reporters, who are less obtrusive and need only a pad, a pen and a phone.

Not all the inadequacies of television coverage are of Chinese making; some begin with editorial decisions made back home. Before Tiananmen, the political story was sometimes a hard one to sell. Any script containing more than a couple of Chinese names was considered too confusing for viewers. What editors preferred were pictures, which China provides in abundance. Hence the clichéd stories: stockpiles of cabbage each winter in Beijing and the new restaurant serving rats in Guangzhou, rosy-cheeked children bundled up for school and old folks doing Taiqi in the Shanghai dawn. These often run as 'kickers', the cute item that comes on after all the bad news and ends the show on a happy note. Although such stories make good television, they too often tend to reinforce the simplistic stereotype of 'eccentric Chinese' at the expense of more important stories. Happily, after Tiananmen, the domestic appetite is changing.

Language is another barrier for television. There are far fewer Chinese speakers in television than in print. Since networks move their on-air correspondents from post to post, they are seldom willing to commit the time or money for language training. Many reporters who do speak Mandarin originally went to China to study and later moved into journalism; others are Sinophiles who have been on the beat for a long time. But these groups tend to work for newspapers. The language problem means that television cannot get as close to the story. It relies more on translators, and those supplied by the government tend to discourage contact with sources who have anything controversial to say.

All these factors came into play, and made coverage that much more difficult, when the tanks moved into Tiananmen Square. From the beginning, it was a story made for television; and television was there in strength. The international media circus had pitched its tent to cover the visit of Mikhail Gorbachev. But he quickly became a sideshow; the main event was the student takeover of Tiananmen Square. The Chinese authorities, sticking at first with their policy of more openness, allowed it to be covered.

The dazzling tableau of Tiananmen Square was great television; the world was riveted by the defiance of student leaders and the courage of hunger strikers. More complicated issues were addressed – who these students were, what they wanted and how they hoped to succeed without wider support from workers and peasants – but the basic plot for television was simple. These were brave, young underdogs against ageing autocrats, good guys in white hats against villains in black.

The same scenes were played over and over again around the world: the Goddess of Democracy rising in dappled sunshine, then toppled in a sombre dawn; thousands of students challenging their rulers, then only one standing defiantly in front of a line of tanks. Those are the snapshots that television burned into the world's conscience.

Television could not and did not tell the whole story of Tiananmen Square and its aftermath. The medium's traditional failings – that it sensationalizes and oversimplifies – are exaggerated in China, even more so during crises. It provides the snapshots, but not always the context that is more easily obtained, explained and analysed by print. A picture is not always worth a thousand well-chosen words.

Yet fewer people take the time these days to read those thousand words. The ability to transmit live coverage from almost anywhere in the world does give television an immediacy that newspapers cannot match, as coverage of the Gulf war has shown. Television provided the most enduring images of China's democracy movement and the assault that stifled it on 4 June.

Playing to the camera

It has been argued that the media, especially television, also provided the 'oxygen of publicity' that fuelled the students' revolt. Lee Kuan Yew, the former prime minister of Singapore, argued that the students were naively encouraged to emulate uprisings in the Philippines and South Korea.

Because their television viewing was contextless [he told the Commonwealth Press Union in October 1990], China's students forgot that China was a very different country from the Philippines or South Korea, two countries with close links to the United States where the media and congress wield immense influence.

The Chinese students were euphoric when the groundswell of support for them was shown world-wide on television. Encouraged by feedback from Chinese students abroad, they pressed on hoping to achieve something as dramatic as the changes in the Philippines and South Korea. But the ending was different.

What had happened in Burma in 1988 was real bullets and real deaths as a result of mass demonstrations. But the Chinese students never saw this on television because there were no television crews to record these clashes in Burma.

Lee's belief that the students should have been more patient in seeking reform probably reflects his interest in discouraging protest in Singapore. He does, however, raise the question of whether the presence of cameras influenced events and contributed to the ugly ending. There were specific incidents when that may have been true. For example, on the morning before the final assault, demonstrators had blocked several thousand soldiers on their initial foray into the city. We found one car, with a senior officer in the front seat, surrounded by crowds. As we filmed, a man looked our way, then reached through the window and punched the officer in the face. We felt he did it because we were filming, that our presence could encourage more violence. We stopped filming and backed off. But that is just one incident. To question how the presence of cameras influenced the wider events over several weeks is a theoretical exercise; it is impossible to imagine such events in a media vacuum. Television did focus naturally on the forces for democracy. It had little access to the power struggle among Chinese leaders. The students were more accessible and more compelling. Their demonstrations dominated coverage. But the students originally timed their protest more to Gorbachev's visit than to the presence of the media. They may have seen foreign reporters as political allies, drawn encouragement from their presence and believed that cameras afforded some kind of protection. Yet the media had neither the time nor the taste for philosophical debates on their role; hands were full just trying to keep up with a huge, complicated story. Certainly our reports and others detailed the divisions and confusion among student leaders, the risks they ran and the potential for violence. By late May, student leader Wu'er Kaixi, with all his antics, had almost as many media critics as Li Peng. If the students did naively draw too much encouragement from the media, there was little the media could do to stop them.

Getting on the air

At first, it was possible to film the student occupation of Tiananmen Square and to satellite the pictures through Chinese facilities or from dishes set up by the networks themselves. After the declaration of martial law, satellite transmissions were stopped, and it was made illegal to film in the streets. We all continued to film anyway because no one seemed to be enforcing the ban, probably because of the uncertainty resulting from the power struggle among Chinese leaders. But, after the assault on the square, we were hard-pressed to do any reporting at all. Chinese authorities did not cut phone lines or ask us to leave, despite constant rumours that they would. But intimidation escalated, and the satellite ban continued – the only time it was lifted was the night they announced that Jiang Zemin had replaced Zhao Ziyang as party boss, a message they wanted to get out to the world.

The lack of satellite transmissions was an immense obstacle; to get around it, we had to innovate. On the Monday after the Tiananmen assault, there was shooting on Changan Avenue near the Beijing Hotel and in the streets around the diplomatic compound at Jianguomenwai. Chinese were shot in the streets; diplomats and their families ducked for cover. My cameraman and I were in the compound that morning when the shooting broke out. We filmed foreign families hiding behind cars as Chinese soldiers shot from passing trucks. Those pictures were carried to Hong Kong that afternoon by a 'pigeon' – someone willing to risk carrying a tape out on their flight. The tape was delivered to a television news service office in Hong Kong and then satellited to our head office in Toronto. Our office also received pictures from Monday night's Chinese newscast, which detailed the government's version of what had happened over the past weekend — that rebels and thugs had attacked and killed brave soldiers. Those pictures were picked off satellites, recorded in Hong Kong, then sent round the world.

By Monday evening, Toronto time, our head office had received both our pictures and the Chinese newscast in time for the main newscast at 11 p.m. But we were 12 hours ahead in Beijing. When I woke up at 6 a.m. on Tuesday, it was still five hours before our Monday night newscast. I telephoned my editor to discuss the latest developments as reported on international news-wires and to talk about what should be in my report. I then wrote a script to marry to the pictures available in Toronto. The American network ABC, with whom we shared most of a floor at the Great Wall Sheraton, had set up a special telephone with satellite-quality sound. Using that line, I read my script to Toronto, where an editor added pictures.

Much of our coverage was *ad hoc*, a patchwork job, and the complications were immense. Tapes were sometimes lost. Editors didn't always understand what pictures went with which words. Late news developments didn't always match the video available. Television coverage has been criticized as confusing and sensationalist. In fact it is a miracle that television crews managed to get as much as they did on the air.

In light of television coverage of Tiananmen Square, networks came up with new strategies. In Romania, for example, ITN erected a portable satellite dish and a satellite phone on the roof of a Timisoara hotel so that they could transmit pictures directly to London. During the Gulf war, Bob McKoewn of CBS was the first to transmit from Kuwait City; he sent out his scoop on a suitcase-size dish. It is still possible for Chinese authorities to limit access to the outside world, but perhaps not as easily as in 1989.

Disappearing sources

Another problem was lack of information. After Tiananmen, the truth was brutalized. Students were in hiding; the government had the field to itself and repeatedly broadcast its twisted story of thugs and counter-revolutionary rebels killing soldiers. Few dared to tell the other side of the story; fewer still were willing to tell it on television. Correspondents felt compelled to step into the void. This was sometimes a contentious step; the golden rule of journalism is objectivity, and my editors in Toronto wondered at times if I had forgotten it. But when the government alleged that no protestors were killed, that the trouble was started by thugs and rebels, no Chinese was available to say in front of the cameras, 'That's a lie'. Rightly, I think, we had to do that for them. Pure 'objectivity' would have been morally unacceptable.

In the hours and days just after the assault, there were a few people still brave enough to speak out. But the Chinese put an end to that with a most sinister kind of intimidation. The American network ABC interviewed a Chinese man who told of seeing people killed. Chinese authorities got hold of that interview, perhaps by monitoring the newscast in the United States. It was re-broadcast in China, and the man was arrested. The man was made an example; as the old saying goes, kill a chicken to scare the monkeys.

Not only did it deter Chinese from speaking, it also deterred foreign reporters from asking. Many reporters were in the firing line during the assault. Cameras especially were an obvious target. The CBS correspondent, Richard Roth, was attacked by Chinese soldiers and then held incommunicado for almost a day. Undercover thugs, whom we affectionately referred to as 'gooners', attacked me and my crew that night outside the Beijing Hotel. Inside the hotel, they cut telephone lines and confiscated videotapes. Most reporters were willing to risk their own safety, but not the safety of Chinese contacts, who were so much more vulnerable.

In the early hours of Sunday 5 June, before the arrests began, I went to the Capital Hospital, just a few blocks from Tiananmen Square, in search of victims and bodies. Authorities would not let us in, but relatives begged us to keep trying. Finally, a group of sympathetic doctors and nurses pushed aside the guard and let us in through another gate. They fought to get us a key to the morgue to show us the bodies. The halls were lined with the injured; the walls and floors were stained with blood. One nurse cried as she told of the dead bodies she had seen, of the brutality of the soldiers. I wonder now if that nurse, who so honestly and emotionally told us her truth, was later arrested.

In the next few weeks, our camera crew was detained several times by police or soldiers for filming in the streets. Each time, they spent less time questioning the foreigners among us than they did our Chinese interpreter and our Chinese driver. The intimidation worked well on them and even better on us. Not wanting to put the innocent at risk, we resorted to moving around the city without Chinese help. We used a home video camera instead of our more obvious professional one. Our job became ever more difficult.

Unfortunately, Western diplomats were not always as useful as they might have been in taking up the slack and countering Chinese disinformation. Many were evacuated to Hong Kong just when they were needed most in Beijing; others were as uncertain as the reporters they sought to advise.

One example took place on the day that the tanks moved out of Tiananmen Square and took up a position at the roundabout in front of the diplomatic compound at Jianguomenwai. There were hints, reinforced by diplomats, that troops loyal to Zhao Ziyang were moving in from the east to do battle with troops who had taken the square. My cameraman and I took over an evacuated flat to film the military deployment throughout one very nervous night. The next day, a foreign military analyst looked at our pictures. He suggested that the tanks had taken up a defensive position and that roads were being mined. Two weeks later, he brought two of his colleagues from other embassies to watch that same video. They agreed the troops were not in a defensive position and were not mining the road. The media, they said, had got it wrong. The media did occasionally get it wrong, sometimes because they relied on 'Western diplomatic sources'.

One diplomatic contact told me within a couple of days of the assault that, according to his sources, troops loyal to Zhao had in fact quietly taken over the square and were waiting for Zhao's triumphant return. That 'story' seemed preposterous, could not be confirmed and, thankfully, was not reported. But it's an example of the kind of wild rumour that found life in the information vacuum. For a reporter, caution was an essential rule, although the pressure to file something that made sense of all the conflicting accounts sometimes made it a hard one to live by.

Many diplomats did brave the streets during the Tiananmen assault, and provided useful insights and information throughout my posting in China. But reports based on 'Western diplomatic sources' should always be viewed with caution; diplomats in China can be wrong as often as the media can.

Taking stock

With few eyewitnesses and fewer facts, the question of how many died at Tiananmen became a controversial and unresolved issue. From the horror of 4 June sprang reports of hundreds, perhaps thousands, dead. The International Red Cross in Beijing was initially quoted as putting the death toll at 2,400, a report it later denied. There were reports, based on the sight of smoke rising in Tiananmen Square, that soldiers were burning bodies. Since the government insisted that only about three dozen civilians died, the second-guessing began. Nick Kristoff of the *New York Times*, who later won a Pulitzer Prize, calculated that 'only 800 died'. That led to the question of whether there really was a massacre. For those of us who'd seen some of the carnage, such questions seemed a repulsive red herring. What is a massacre? Is 2,400 dead a massacre, but 800 not? Would it not be a massacre if soldiers killed 80 or even 18 unarmed citizens?

It is true that television did not come up with enough shots of dead bodies to provide firm evidence of the numbers killed. There may be several reasons for that. Most crews were positioned in the square that night; there were fewer at Muxidi, in western Beijing, site of some of the most violent initial confrontations. Some crews apparently left the square for their own safety when the shooting began; others, like the CBS crew, were prevented from filming. As for our crew, after the initial incident at Jianguomenwai, it was virtually impossible to penetrate the security cordon to get back into the square. We concentrated instead on getting shots of the dead and injured being carried out.

The numbers issue provided a lesson for all reporters: don't get carried away in the heat of the moment; be cautious about body counts. The lesson was useful just six months later when protestors in Romania exaggerated the number killed in Timisoara in an effort to increase the international outrage against the Ceausescu regime. Any unsubstantiated reporting can be used as ammunition by authoritarian governments to try to undermine the credibility of all reporting.

More generally, television's record at Tiananmen was mixed. Pressures of round-the-clock demands on a round-the-clock story were made even more severe by the difference in time between Beijing and home base. Reporters were constantly tied to the telephone or to the edit suite; there was not enough time to get into the streets, even less to sit back and assess. Increasing fatigue muddied minds and occasionally reports. And, as it became more difficult to film in the streets, the pictures dried up and so did the interest back home. Despite achievements, television had neither the ability nor the tenacity of print to stick with the story, to get behind it, and to find out what really happened.

9

The winds that keep blowing: China and its foreign press corps since June 1989

SIMON LONG

Maybe it is the fate of the foreign media in China always to get it wrong. Despite being charged with responsibility for the way the world was caught off guard by the Chinese leadership's brutality in June 1989, the media may still, even now, be leaving outsiders ill-prepared for the next turning-point in modern Chinese history. Certainly that is what China's official ideologues believe, with the refinement that they also accuse the foreign media of trying to bring about that turning-point through their own efforts. On 12 June 1991, *People's Daily* published a signed commentary attacking the activities of 'a small number of foreigners' in Beijing. Aimed principally at foreign journalists, and especially at those working for the BBC and Voice of America radio stations, it accused them of trying to foment unrest to mark the second anniversary of the Beijing massacre on 4 June, and gloated over their failure. 'The winds that keep blowing though the trees want to be still,' it was entitled. 'Watch the Performance of a Small Number of Foreigners.'

The background to the commentary was the demonstration that took place at Beijing University one year earlier, on the first anniversary of the massacre – the one sizeable outbreak of political unrest that has occurred in Beijing since. Many foreign journalists had been caught unawares by the several-hundred-strong gathering. Access to campus was difficult, especially after road-blocks, manned by uniformed police and plain-clothes thugs, virtually sealed off the university district of Haidian. Of the few reporters who were on the spot, a number were beaten up by security personnel. A year later, foreign reporters were better prepared. There was a small demonstration. The implication of the *People's Daily* article was that it had been provoked by the presence of two dozen expectant journalists. It is undeniable that the presence of the reporters may at least have encouraged the small number of protestors. *People's Daily* noted gleefully, however, that 'Western press agencies finally had to report that Beijing was "quiet" and "without incident".'

The article finished with the sombre warning that 'attempts by anyone to change the choice and will of the Chinese people will be futile'. This hints at the official view of the foreign media. We were seen as important warriors in the West's campaign of 'peaceful evolution' – that is, the 'war without gunpowder' to subvert socialism in China. We were obsessed by human rights, political prisoners and the 4 June massacre, despite being told by Prime Minister Li Peng, at the annual prime ministerial conference in April 1991, that that was 'history'. Why were we not reporting China's great achievements in 'opening up, reform and economic construction'?, officials would ask.

Mr Li was wrong about 4 June – still the single most important, and in some senses the only, issue in Chinese politics. However, there is a grain of truth in the criticism that Western press coverage of China is dominated by issues related to the Beijing massacre and its aftermath. There may also be justice in the implication that this is giving the outside world the wrong impression of China. The contention of this chapter, however, is that the wrong impression given in fact bolsters myths fostered by the Beijing leadership itself. Despite their mutually antagonistic relationship since June 1989, Beijing propagandists and the foreign press are both perpetuating a number of dubious notions about the nature of contemporary Chinese society and politics.

Before examining these 'dubious notions' themselves, I shall turn to three areas in which I consider there are major contributory factors in the misrepresentation I am alleging. They are: the practical problems of reporting in China; the role now played by the foreign media in Chinese politics; and the relationship between Beijing-based correspondents and their editorial offices or news desks at home.

The difficulties of reporting in China

By far the biggest single difficulty in reporting from China is the obsessive secrecy of the political system. This is too often taken for granted. Is it not extraordinary, for example, that nobody even knows who is the most important politician in China? In May 1989, Zhao Ziyang, then communist party leader, disclosed in a meeting with Mikhail Gorbachev in Beijing that in 1987 the politburo had passed a secret resolution requiring that all important matters should be referred to Deng Xiaoping, now notionally retired. It is still not known whether that resolution has been rescinded. Asked about it in April 1991, Li Peng was evasive. He said that Mr Deng was 'encouraging' Mr Li and his colleagues to be 'more independent and mature', but was still, like other octogenarian veterans, a source of advice.

At a more mundane level, secrecy is manifest in the ban on 'telephone interviews' with officials. In other words, the normal journalistic practice of calling an official for clarification or comment is in theory not allowed, although the ban is only patchily enforced. Interview requests must pass through the 'foreign affairs bureau' of the department concerned. Usually they are turned down. When they take place, they are generally no more enlightening than a reading of the official press. The spark of interest fired by a response beginning 'In my personal opinion' is invariably followed by a statement that comes word for word from the latest *People's Daily* editorial or party circular.

Meanwhile, the deliberations of the most important organs of state and party are held in camera, and revealed only in uninformative communiqués. The official media operate under the fiction that there is stability and harmony among Chinese politicians, and hence inevitable differences over policy must be decoded in the arcane cryptography of China-watching, just as during the dark days of the Cultural Revolution.

Yet, for official opinion and even fact, the foreign correspondent is forced back on the media, which are avowedly propagandist. 'Stability is the overriding concern,' said Li Ruihuan, politburo member in charge of propaganda, in December 1989. 'The crucial matter is that, in news reporting, the principle of giving prominence to positive propaganda should be upheld.' On the whole, his wishes have been followed. A major uprising by Islamic ethnic minorities in the western region of Xinjiang the following April was not reported at all in China's national media, and it was a fortnight before even the regional press, which few outside the area see, mentioned the incident. Even plane crashes are reported only if there are foreign casualties.

At times, it has seemed as if the press has gone back a quarter of a century. There are the same mind-numbing editorials; the same mechanical reporting of the leadership's travels; the same relentless triumphalism at any piece of good news – a good harvest or a satellite launch.

The pages of the newspapers are even peopled by many of the same characters as in the early 1960s. Both the long-lived leaders still battling for power – and still worrying about where their photographs appear in *People's Daily* – and the same semi-mythical cult heroes for people to emulate. For party officials, there is the model cadre Jiao Yulu from the 1960s; for workers there is his contemporary, the Stakhanovite Iron Man, Wang Jinxi; for soldiers there is Lei Feng, the humble, complaisant boy-scout squaddie. At least the children have a new model: the teenager Lai Ning, who died in 1989 fighting a forest fire with her own body.

Despite this, China's press has certainly not reverted to the straitjacket of the Cultural Revolution. Partly, this is simply a matter of volume. There are now 1,600 newspapers and 3,000 'social science publications', mostly fairly vividly written magazines. And the press delights in anecdotes of the 'believe it or not' variety – the lost tribe in the Taklamaklan desert, out of contact with civilization for 300 years; the masturbating boy whose penis burst into flames; the man who bought a wife who turned out to be a man; the dumpling stall which acquired its meat by buying human buttocks from the local mortuary; and so on. Many such stories are palpably false. They are reported by foreign news agencies, however, because they are given a spurious authenticity by their appearance in 'the official Chinese media'.

This begs an obvious question. If we cannot believe the Chinese press about the incendiary effects of masturbation, why should we believe it about the 'stability and unity' of Chinese politics?

However, fortunately for the transparency of Chinese politics, the system is increasingly leaky. For example, a series of internal party documents that since 1989 have berated Mikhail Gorbachev for betraying socialism, while the public media refrained from comment and applauded improvements in relations with Moscow, found their way into the hands of the foreign press. In some cases, the leaks may have been officially inspired. But, in a warning to foreign journalists that possession of such documents was a 'breach of regulations', the London *Independent*'s Beijing correspondent, Andrew Higgins, was expelled from China in September 1991 after being found with a copy of an internal party circular on unrest in Inner Mongolia.

The secrecy is enforced by surveillance and harassment of the Beijing press corps. This has been stepped up since June 1989. The Beijing Foreign Correspondents' Club, an unofficial self-help organization that is unrecognized by the authorities, has repeatedly protested to the Foreign Ministry. One such protest in February 1990 read as follows:

In the last few months, many foreign correspondents have been followed by Chinese security agents in the streets of Beijing, and some of our Chinese friends have been interrogated because they dare to see us. The surveillance has noticeably increased in the last two weeks. There is no other place in the world today where foreign correspondents are subject to such intense, systematic harassment as we are in China.

Specific cases of this harassment include the following recent examples:

– Three Chinese citizens who visited the residence of a European correspondent last week were taken away by security agents as they left the building, which is located in a foreign diplomatic compound. They were subsequently interrogated for nearly one hour.

– A North American journalist reports that he is now routinely followed, even while jogging near his home and travelling to a recent meeting of the Foreign Correspondents' Club at the Sheraton Great Wall Hotel.

– Chinese security agents have followed a European journalist to meetings with Chinese friends on numerous occasions and attempted to surreptitiously photograph and record the meetings, using a camera that was partially concealed in a dummy attaché case.

– Other correspondents report that their friends have been confronted by leaders of their work units, who told them that their meetings with foreign journalists have been monitored by Chinese security agents and must cease at once.

We most strongly object to this interference in the journalistic work of accredited foreign correspondents, which is plainly being carried out by agencies and/or departments of the Chinese government.

We request a meeting with you and with representatives of relevant security organizations at the earliest possible date to discuss this urgent situation. We hope you will agree that it is vitally important – not only for us but also for the reputation of the Chinese government – that immediate steps be taken to halt these attempts to intimidate and obstruct our normal and lawful professional and social contacts with Chinese citizens.

Sincerely,
JAMES MUNSON
President

The Ministry of Foreign Affairs responded that the allegations were without foundation, and that journalists were being 'over-sensitive'. They were, however, a fairly routine catalogue of some aspects of the life-style of a foreign correspondent in China. They do not include unverifiable but highly probable forms of surveillance, such as the tapping and taping of telephone calls, the interception of mail, and the questioning of Chinese members of staff about the activities of their foreign employers.

The role of the foreign media in Chinese politics
One paradoxical effect of the pattern of harassment outlined in James Munson's letter is that many foreign reporters have far better dissident sources than official access. Since the very act of talking to a foreign journalist may lay one open to interrogation by one's employers or the security forces, those who make an effort to maintain contact are often those who are already excluded from the political system.

This in turn is one reason for the deployment of such extensive official resources for keeping an eye on foreign reporters. They are, of course, important in China's efforts to burnish its international image. But, as demonstrated by the decision to send tanks into central Beijing under the eyes of the world's media in June 1989, that is a lesser consideration.

What foreigners write about China has an exaggerated importance in the eyes of China's leaders, not so much for the impact abroad as because of its domestic effects. Foreign news comes in through foreign radio broadcasts, especially the BBC and Voice of America. The Chinese language transmissions of both networks have been jammed in Beijing since late 1989, but half-heartedly or incompetently. Despite official attempts to denigrate the broadcasts, especially those of Voice of America, they enjoy widespread popular respect as being more reliable than China's own media. Also, according to the Chinese *Fortnightly Chat Yearbook*, the newspaper with the largest print run in China is not *People's Daily* (2.8 million) but the internal *Reference News* (3.3 million), which reprints foreign newspaper and news agency reports. The reports are doctored and highly selective, especially where China is concerned. Of my own articles, for example, I saw reprinted in *Reference News* one on the hordes of Russian and East European shoppers flocking to Beijing, and one on the economy which noted how price inflation had been brought under control (the bulk of my piece, on the unemployment this had brought, was not reprinted).

This unwarranted importance of the foreign media is enhanced by their role as an outlet for those with grievances to air against the authorities. Failed petitioners, would-be émigrés and the dwindling community of openly dissident intellectuals all on occasion turn to foreign journalists for help. And once a year, at the prime minister's press conference, televised live nationwide, foreign journalists become famous for thirty seconds, or however long it takes them to pose their question. To see the prime minister treated like a politician in a Western country is a unique experience for many Chinese viewers. For some journalists, it is hard to remember that they are reporters, not representatives of an oppressed nation, with no such privileged access to their oppressor.

The correspondents' relationship with head office

Fame for thirty seconds became especially beguiling after China fell off the world's news map in 1990–91. For all the horror and, in some cases, personal danger that foreign reporters experienced during the Beijing massacre, it was for many their finest hour professionally. Many are sinologists by training. All those years spent learning characters, those miserable winters studying on godforsaken Chinese campuses, those years learning their journalistic craft in menial jobs, had at least brought a moment in the limelight.

In the summer of 1989, I returned to London, before going back to Beijing in September. In meetings with editors at headquarters, I encountered a kind of party line. 'We used not to take China seriously,' it would go, with an explanation of how they used to like stories along the lines of 'Look! The Chinese go disco dancing! Play snooker! Eat Kentucky Fried Chicken!' and so on. But from now on, I was told, China was a serious political story.

In the next two years, I wrote and broadcast around a million words on China, the majority covering this 'serious political story'. When I came back in the autumn of 1991, I had the impression that the only two pieces anyone recalled were about, respectively, the sex-life of the Giant Panda, and a purported breakthrough in penis enlargement techniques. What had gone wrong?

The first problem was the unprecedented extent of 'foreign' news for readers in Western Europe, the United States and Japan. June 1989 was not a climactic event, but merely the first in a series of astonishing developments all over the world. The Berlin Wall came down, governments in Eastern Europe crumbled, Iraq invaded Kuwait and the world went to war, and the Soviet Union disintegrated.

Meanwhile, in China, what happened? In November 1989, Deng Xiaoping announced his resignation from his last official posts. But we had been describing him as 'notionally retired' since 1987, and did not believe him now either. In January 1990, martial law was lifted in Beijing, but we dismissed it as a 'cosmetic' move. In September 1990, the biggest international event ever staged in China was held in Beijing. But few people in the West could get excited about the Asian Games. In early 1991, Tiananmen activists were put on trial, but there was a war in the Gulf. In the summer of 1991, there was serious flooding in large parts of China. But there is every year.

After their couple of months basking on the front pages, Beijing correspondents found themselves scrambling for space in inside columns. Some grew dispirited. Many editors in fact would claim that they have been exceptionally loyal to 'the China story', despite its obstinate refusal to move. However, since 1989, there has been a clear perception of what that 'story' is – one of continuing political repression, and of whether communism can hold out in one of its last bastions. That story has, for the time being, gone off the boil.

Five myths about China
It is my contention that the impression a general reader would take away from following China in the newspapers since 1989 matches in many respects one that the Chinese Communist Party would want to convey, and is false. I would summarize this into five central myths about China promulgated by the Beijing authorities: (a) that China is a socialist country; (b) that the Chinese Communist Party is a strong central government; (c) that 'the third generation of leaders with Jiang Zemin at its core is stable and united'; (d) that economic growth is conducive to political stability; and (e) that China never compromises on issues affecting its internal affairs. Because of their importance to our perception of contemporary China, it is appropriate to examine each in turn in some detail:

(a) China is a socialist country
China is of course a socialist country, in the sense that the term is used now — it is a repressive, one-party dictatorship whose rulers avow Marxist/Leninist principles. However, the use of the words 'socialist' or 'communist' carries with it a big bundle of historical baggage, implying that the political system has far more to do with Marxism than is the case. In early 1991, China published a 'Ten-Year Programme' (TYP) outlining economic strategy to the year 2000. The plan was cautious and quite conservative. Nevertheless, if it is followed, by 2000, China will no

longer be a socialist country – even as the communist party itself defines the term. There are two types of definition:

(i) *Political*. Asked, 'What is socialism?', Chinese officials will reply with the tautological formulation put forward in 1980 by Deng Xiaoping. Socialism means the Four Basic Principles, namely: the Socialist Road; Marxism-Leninism-Mao Zedong Thought; the People's Democratic Dictatorship; and the leading role of the communist party. Chinese leaders habitually stress that the fourth 'principle' – party leadership – is the most important. In other words, socialism's most important feature is that the communist party is an unchallenged power.

(ii) *Economic*. Clearly, if the party can continue as effectively as it has since 1989 to suppress dissent, there is no obvious reason why, in 2000, China will not be a socialist country by this definition. However, this is plainly not adequate to explain what distinguishes socialism as superior to capitalism, so there is in addition an economic definition, relating to the 'socialist' nature of China's 'planned commodity economy'. Socialism is an economic system in which 'public ownership predominates'.

Again, there is at first sight no reason why this need be contradicted by economic developments in the next decade. Agricultural land will still be in public ownership, albeit largely leased on up to 30-year terms to farmers. And, on projections based on the TYP, private industry will still account for only 7 per cent of industrial output by value. The rest will still be in 'public ownership'.

However, this is a fiction, for two reasons. First, the continued success of agricultural reform relies on farmers acting as if they have rights to private land. Not only is there likely to be a shift towards bigger 'private' farms, where economies of scale can offset the problems of low productivity, soil erosion and poor technical inputs, but also, even on small farms, landholders will be required to believe that it is 'their' land.

Second, extrapolating the TYP's sanguine view of growth prospects suggests that, by the year 2000, state-owned enterprises will contribute only 44 per cent of industrial output. Of the balance, 45 per cent will be in 'public ownership' in the form of collectives, but it is misleading to lump these in the same basket. Not only are an unknown number 'disguised' private enterprises; the vast majority are owned by lower-level township or village cooperatives, operate outside the state plan, and are in competition with each other and with the state sector. They are operating in a market, indistinguishable from private enterprises except in the bureaucratic restraints they face. Hence, of total Gross National Product, no more than 37 per cent will be truly in the hands of the state.

The problem of definition is not just an abstruse theoretical debate. The communist party bases its legitimacy on its claim to be the faithful interpreter and adaptor of a body of correct doctrine. 'Without the communist party, there would be no new China,' as its favourite ditty goes. But, in the early 1990s, the party faces the question, 'Without communism, can there be a communist party?'.

Communism, after all, is not a Chinese invention. Despite the adaptations by Mao Zedong and Deng to Chinese reality, it is a body of thought of universal application. If it is true in China, it must also be true elsewhere. Which is why it is worrying for the Chinese leaders that so many of their fellows are abandoning Marxism, or losing power.

The problem is compounded by the reality of China today. Buried away in the columns of *People's Daily*, and more particularly of provincial newspapers, are daily reports of executions, possibly running at tens of thousands a year, as part of a campaign against crime, launched in 1988, called 'the serious onslaught'. The campaign acknowledges what everybody in China knows: that crime is becoming ever more widespread; that corruption is endemic; and that the 'social evils' which the communists had long boasted of eradicating are thriving. Corruption is probably the most serious single threat to party legitimacy. 'Official corruption' was one of the targets of the 1989 protests, and one for which the authorities admitted some justification. It has, by most anecdotal accounts, got worse since. There is probably no commodity, no public service and no official approval that cannot be acquired through the right mixture of cash, cigarettes and 'connections'. China is too vast, too bureaucratic and too inefficient, and corruption has become the accepted way of getting things done.

The collapse of moral values evidenced by the inexorable spread of corruption has also led more and more people to turn to crime; petty theft, armed robbery and murder are all on the increase. The railway network has been prey to marauding bandits; even military bases have seen huge 'wastage' of materials; the power of the criminal gangs, the 'triads', was revealed when it emerged that they had played a leading role in spiriting out of China some of the 'most-wanted' student leaders and dissidents after Tiananmen. Just as alarming is the reappearance of the 'Six Evils', which the communist party claimed to have destroyed as feudal remnants. They are: prostitution, rampant in many areas; gambling, again a national obsession; pornography; drug abuse, resurgent again especially in the southwestern areas close to the 'Golden Triangle'; profiting from feudal superstition, targeted at mountebanks, quack doctors and others pandering to hopes for miracle cures or eternal life; and the abduction and sale of women and children, a nationwide scandal affecting tens of thousands of women sold as wives to farmers who find it cheaper to buy a wife, as they would cattle, than go through the expense and palaver of a traditional wedding.

Clearly, none of this has anything to do with 'socialism' as the party understands it. The failure to stop the spread of corruption, crime and malpractice is evidence both of the party's loss of actual power, and of the disintegration of its moral authority. And yet, in the simplifying shorthand to which the journalist is forced to resort, China is 'a socialist country'.

(b) The Chinese Communist Party is a strong central government
The Chinese Communist Party bases its appeal for support in large measure on the contention that, without its role as a strong central government, there would be chaos and even civil war. 'Without the strong leadership of the communist party, new turmoil and wars would arise and the nation would be split', was one typical formulation, expressed in a *People's Daily* editorial. Because of the foreign media's emphasis on its extraordinarily successful record of political repression nationwide, the communist party's claim to be a strong central government is broadly accepted. It is, however, wrong. Under Deng Xiaoping, central government revenue as a proportion of total national income has dropped from about 70 per cent to about 20 per cent.

The history of economic policy since an austerity programme was introduced in the autumn of 1988 has been in part that of a losing battle waged by planners in Beijing for the re-centralization of economic decision-making, and in part a redistribution of government assets in Beijing's favour. In the nervous political consensus that followed the Beijing massacre, the centre appeared to be winning. It regained control of the distribution of a number of commodities, reinforced restrictions on provincial government spending, and, through the People's Bank, used access to credit as a means of forcing provincial industry to slow down. However, by mid-1991, the extent to which a number of provinces, especially on the southeastern seaboard, had shrugged off the austerity programme to resume very rapid rates of economic growth suggested that the political consensus had been more crucial in the government's success than its control of macroeconomic levers. This had followed the failure in late 1990 to force the provinces into revenue-sharing arrangements with Beijing that were more favourable to the central government. There are at present at least five different sorts of financial arrangement between Beijing and the provinces. The most important are the lump-sum contribution system employed – and jealously guarded – in Guangdong, which leaves the province the benefits of excess growth, and the proportional system used in, for example, Shanghai, which in the 1980s saw as much as 80 per cent of municipal revenues disappear to the capital.

Provincial leaders have clout because of their membership on the party's top decision-making body, the Central Committee. As a body, they have votes enough to affect party policy, and the politburo cannot ride roughshod over their views. Provincial leaders are not just trying to get on with it without central interference; they are turning China into a patchwork of radically different, and in many cases competing, economies.

Short of another major political upset, this is a trend that is likely to grow, especially in the south, as Fujian forges closer links with Taiwan, and Guangdong with Hong Kong. Even ahead of Hong Kong's formal reversion to China in 1997, the degree of economic symbiosis with Guangdong is impressive. Some two million workers there are employed in Hong Kong-funded enterprises. Indeed, Hong Kong's future prosperity probably relies less on who is in power in Beijing than on the continuation of Guangdong's ability to keep its distance from the capital politically as well as geographically. Recent evidence suggests that its chances are high. Meanwhile, separatist tensions in Tibet and Xinjiang are also likely to increase. They will be ruthlessly repressed. But the communist party's durability elsewhere relies less on political coercion than on the free hand it is giving the ethnic Chinese provinces to go their own way. Many believe that the alternative to the communist party is chaos, and if the price of keeping it in power is paying lip-service to an outmoded ideology, it seems quite cheap. But it is not central government strength that is preserving party power.

(c) 'The third generation of leaders with Jiang Zemin at its core is stable and united'

The most frequent question I have faced about China since returning is, 'What will happen when Deng Xiaoping dies?' The implication is that that might be the spark which inspires millions to take to the streets again. But that is only one possibility. And it betrays a misconception that Chinese politics is about a struggle between 'communists' and 'democrats'. Just as probable is that the next battle, like previous ones, will be between different stripes of 'communist'. Because of the intense secrecy with which it is shrouded, the power struggle at the top of Chinese politics is almost impossible to report. Yet we know from official Chinese accounts published retrospectively that the struggle was unceasing in the period from 1921, when the party was founded, up to 1989. There is no reason to believe that it has stopped now.

One of the slogans of the 1989 democracy movement was for the replacement of China's system of 'Rule by Man' with 'Rule by Law'. This was a well-aimed barb. China's politics has relied on there being an 'emperor', a final arbiter of factional squabbles, who, regardless of his formal position or title, carried the role of 'senior leader'. This was the role Mao played; his death in 1976 sparked a period of profound political uncertainty, until Deng Xiaoping emerged as the clear successor. Mr Deng turns 88 in August 1992. He cannot live for ever, and the Chinese political system will have to cope again with the tension between 'Rule by Man' and the laws of nature.

But since Deng's 'retirement' from his last official posts, the picture has been muddied. He has deliberately withdrawn from the public eye. At times this is rumoured to be due to ill health. But it also accords with a strategy of trying to build up the image and credibility of the 'third generation', and especially of its 'core', Jiang Zemin, the latest in an apparently doomed line of Deng's anointed successors. Thus, at the height of Chinese politics there now appears to be a three-tier structure.

Notionally in control are Jiang Zemin, Prime Minister Li Peng and their four fellow members of the politburo Standing Committee. These represent what has become a standard balance between 'reformist' and 'conservative' forces. Joining Jiang in the 'reformist' camp is Li Ruihuan. Like Jiang, Li was promoted in June 1989 as part of the coalition hastily cobbled together to restore a semblance of order after the massacre. Like Jiang, too, Li was a mayor of an 'open' coastal city – Tianjin in his case (Jiang has been mayor and subsequently communist party leader in Shanghai). Li Peng, a conservative, is bolstered by two veterans of the central planning system, Yao Yilin and Song Ping. Standing somewhere in the middle is Qiao Shi, the head of the party's internal security apparatus, and apparently a protégé of the aged but robust constitutional expert Peng Zhen.

The most visible of the generation of octogenarians still wielding considerable power from behind the scenes is Yang Shangkun – not by virtue of his role as state president, which is largely honorific, but because of his links in the army. Yang may already have stepped into the role of 'senior leader' that he seems destined to assume, should he outlive Deng. And Mr Yang, born in 1908, seems very robust.

But while he lives, Mr Deng (b. 1904) still seems capable of making occasional decisive interventions in politics. Yang Shangkun has never been recorded as saying anything that is novel or interesting, or that has not been said before in a *People's Daily* editorial. Deng, however, is still occasionally reported as uttering gnomic pronouncements (such as 'speed up reform'), which nevertheless become part of the official vocabulary of political rhetoric and have an influence on the direction of politics. It is rather reminiscent of Mao's last months when, despite suffering from Parkinson's disease and often becoming lost in senility, he still muttered or scribbled instructions that had great political import.

So Deng Xiaoping, with the support of Yang Shangkun, seemed – at least until his intervention in the political debate in early 1992 – to be setting the scene for a quiet shuffling off of the mortal coil, when his absence will not matter, and will not lead to an open rift or battle for the succession. However, there are strong indications that consensus has yet to be reached – the failure to fill vacant politburo seats, for example, or to settle the case of the party leader Zhao Ziyang, who was ousted in June 1989. But because of the absence of reliable sources, Western media risk portraying the complex political life of China as monolithic.

(d) Economic growth is conducive to political stability

In contrasting China with Eastern Europe and the former Soviet Union, one of the points most often made is that China's economy has, by comparison, boomed. So, the argument goes, there is not the same degree of disillusionment with the communist party. In fact, the extent of the popular unrest in China in 1989 far exceeded numerically anything seen in Moscow. And that followed a period of exceptionally rapid economic growth. Indeed, each of the three 'high tides' of the economic cycle since 1978 has been accompanied, or shortly followed, by pro-democracy agitation on China's streets. This is not surprising. Periods of rapid economic change naturally engender hopes of political change as well. This has not, in any meaningful sense, been forthcoming. So there is no institutional outlet for political aspirations for change, and people, especially students, take to the streets.

Chinese leaders respond to this dilemma in a variety of ways, but it is important to realize that not one has publicly argued, even since the Beijing massacre, for a repudiation of the reforms. Hardline Marxists, like the vice-president Wang Zhen, may well believe that the open door is inseparable from 'bourgeois liberalization' and for that reason should be closed. But they have not been allowed to say so in public, and they represent a minority view. Most seem genuinely to accept that the reforms represent China's best hope, and differ only over the pace and direction of the reforms, and over the shape of Chinese society at the end of the process – notably over the relative importance of the market and the state in the economy. Deng Xiaoping's major legacy to Chinese politics is the shared assumption that government must prove itself in terms of economic advance. He has de-politicized China. The communist party represents a bankrupt ideological force. China's leaders hang by the thread of economic advance, and for that they need the reforms and the outside world. The old stuff, as Deng so succinctly put it, did not work. But the evidence suggests that the 'new stuff' puts the party out of a job.

So the notion that, with the massacre, economic hardliners regained control and back-tracked on the reforms is a myth. True, some reforms that were discussed before were shelved on ideological grounds, such as the development of stock markets; and, until the Pudong project in Shanghai was approved in April 1991, no major new reforms were announced. But the only real 'back-tracking' was the re-imposition in December 1989 of central government control over the allocation of some commodities. And all of these developments were traceable not to the massacre, but to the agreed response to the 1988 overheating of the economy.

By the end of 1991, the party's rhetoric was uniformly 'reformist' on economic issues. This went largely unnoticed in the West, because it did not fit the 'China story', until Deng himself publicized the reform drive early the next year.

(e) China never compromises on issues affecting its internal affairs and sovereignty

This is a key part of the communist party's self-justification: that it has lifted China to its rightful place at the high table of great powers, after the century of national humiliation that began with the 1840 Opium War. The wrangle in 1990-92 with the United States over China's 'Most Favoured Nation' (MFN) trading status has brought this into focus. China has in fact made a series of significant concessions to the demands of the United States. On human rights it has (or says it has) freed 900 people arrested for their part in the 1989 protests; it has allowed the 'criminal' dissident astrophysicist Fang Lizhi to leave his sanctuary in the US Embassy and emigrate; it has accepted visits from US officials and even international delegations to discuss its 'internal affair' of human rights in China; it has seen to it that those dissidents of most concern to the United States received, by China's lights, lenient prison sentences. On the international scene, it muffled the voices that were saying in internal documents that the Gulf war was part of a bid by the US to control oil supplies as part of a campaign for global domination; it did not use its UN veto to stop the war against Iraq; it has, it claims, stopped arming the Khmer Rouge, and it played an important role in facilitating a Cambodian settlement; it took part in the July 1991 US-convened Paris meeting of the UN permanent five on curbing arms sales to the Middle East. None of these has been presented as a concession. China says it has 'made every effort' to improve relations with the West, but still insists that it does not bow to foreign pressure. China's leaders see themselves as victims of a US-led plot to topple them from power. After all, senior US spokesmen say so themselves, when they argue that extending the MFN status offers the best hope of effecting peaceful democratic change in China.

China resents President Bush's New World Order, which it suspects of being a Pax Americana. But it has yet to adapt to the post-cold-war world, to the loss of the leverage it enjoyed during the days of superpower confrontation. China has lost a strategic triangle, and has yet to find a role.

Meanwhile it finds itself dependent on the United States for perhaps a quarter of its export sales, and on the business generated by foreign-funded (largely by Hong Kong and Taiwan) enterprises for one-fifth of its total trade. Since it relies on economic growth not just for its own sake but for its ideological justification as well, it has no option but to make concessions to the outside world.

These concessions have been very important in China's own terms. But they have been trivial in comparison with the reforms elsewhere in the old socialist world. It is their piecemeal and cosmetic nature that interests the foreign media, thereby bolstering the Chinese Communist Party's self-image as the proud party that yields to no foreign bully.

Conclusion

I began by lamenting that the foreign media in China always get it wrong. That is probably fair comment. In every decade since the communist victory in 1949, China has been shaken by an unforeseen political upheaval. Even the relatively open 1980s ended with a shock. I do not intend to criticize those who have reported on China since 1989. I myself, after all, am one of them. I think that, as a group and on the whole, we reported fairly, fully and with commitment to the country and its culture. The point I am making is that China is still subject to a range of preconceptions in the West. June 1989 brought about a dramatic shift in the nature of those preconceptions, but still not all of them are accurate. To state the obvious: China is a huge place in the grip of extraordinarily complex political, social and economic changes. Trying to fit these changes into a pattern of an intelligible 'China story' inevitably leads to simplification and error. The art is not so much to be right, as to be least wrong. And the curious phenomenon is that the foreign media, regarded by Chinese leaders as the advance guard of an imperialist plot to topple them from power, are in fact fostering some of the very myths that the party generates to help it cling to power.

Postscript:
Broadcasting to China

ELIZABETH WRIGHT

Background

The BBC has been broadcasting to China since 1941, when a mere fifteen minutes per week was intended to provide moral support for China in its war against Japan. Recently, we received a letter from a listener in which he said that he first started to listen to us at that time, when he regarded us as a 'beacon of light', and that today, 50 years on, he still regards us as a beacon of light.

That fifteen minutes has now grown to 24.5 hours per week in Mandarin, and 5.25 hours of Cantonese. By early 1993, broadcasts in Mandarin will have increased to 28 hours per week, and the Chinese Service will be one of the largest in the World Service, coming fourth in size after the English-language output, and those in Arabic and Russian.

The BBC's Chinese programmes can be heard in China, Hong Kong, Taiwan, southeast Asia, and, by some quirk of the airwaves, on the west coast of Canada, North and South America, and even as far afield as Brazil. We transmit from Singapore to southeast Asia and central and south China, and from our Hong Kong transmitter to central and north China and northeast Asia. The BBC's Hong Kong transmitter started operations in the autumn of 1987 and transformed the signal in north China, where it was previously extremely weak, into one that was strong and audible. We can be heard all over China, although some areas have better reception than others.

POSTSCRIPT

Why do we broadcast?

Perhaps that question can best be answered by quoting from the World Service Plan, 1991–2: 'Free and untainted information is a basic human right. Not everyone has it; almost everyone wants it. It cannot by itself create a just world, but a just world order can never exist without it.' It is this belief in a free flow of information that is the underlying philosophy of the BBC World Service. Because we are funded by the Foreign and Commonwealth Office, and because it decides the languages in which we broadcast, our relationship with it is often hard for foreigners to understand. It is, perhaps, understandable that the majority of people assume that, since the FCO pays the piper, it must also call the tune, and that our programmes must be a reflection of British foreign policy. However, as our managing director, John Tusa, has said, 'we are makers of programmes and not purveyors of policy'. Again, this is sometimes hard for foreign governments to accept, as it is for some members of their populations, who feel that the BBC 'interferes in our internal affairs'.

In the case of China, the media are not free. Before 1989 we saw a greater liberalization of the print and electronic media. After the Beijing massacre in June 1989 there was, once again, a clampdown. But even before 1989 there were certain subjects that the domestic media approached with extreme caution. Objective analysis of China's own internal political scene was always hard to find, and we know from the thousands of letters which we receive from our listeners that they are particularly interested in western analysis of events in China. However, some listeners have written to say that what happens in China is China's affair, and that we are 'interfering' by speculating on developments there.

Our aim is to provide a broad range of information and analysis about all world developments, including those in China. During the Gulf war, we were quickly made aware of the importance of our broadcasts because, after an initially swift headlining of the start of the war, the Chinese media appear to have received instructions not to give too much coverage to what was happening. It was subsequently left to foreign broadcasting stations to let Chinese listeners know how the war was progressing. We heard from one listener, who was travelling through Sichuan by bus, that the bus-driver had stopped the vehicle and all the passengers had got out and crowded round a short-wave radio to hear our broadcast about the outbreak of the war.

Of even more importance to our listeners was information about the failed Soviet coup in August 1991. Again, the domestic media were quick to report that a coup had taken place, but were much slower off the mark in reporting that it had failed and that Gorbachev had returned to Moscow. We received a great number of letters thanking us for our swift reporting of the events.

What do we broadcast?

Some two-thirds of our output is news and current affairs. Each hour of transmission starts with a nine-minute bulletin, and is followed by between twenty and thirty five minutes of current affairs. The news bulletin comes from the World Service's own newsroom, and the newsreader translates and reads it. The newsroom suggests a range of stories, and we decide which stories to run and in which order. The current affairs broadcast is an analysis of the main stories. Our sources range from despatches from BBC correspondents around the world, through talks written by in-house experts, to interviews in Chinese with experts abroad. We have an increasingly long list of Chinese-speaking interviewees as far afield as Moscow and New York, Hong Kong and Paris. The one country in which it is at present virtually impossible to interview people in Chinese is China itself. We can interview our own correspondent and one or two courageous wives of dissidents, but, despite all our efforts, we have failed to get telephone interviews with officials themselves. We are only too well aware of the importance of providing balance in our output, and greatly regret that it is almost impossible to get the official Chinese view on developments in China, not to mention their attitude towards developments in the rest of the world.

Understandably, our listeners were extremely interested in the collapse of communism in the former Soviet Union and Eastern Europe, and we covered the developments in great depth. We have also followed in similar depth the problems that those countries have encountered in their search for a new political, social and economic order.

But life is not only news and current affairs; we broadcast a very wide range of feature programmes, ranging from arts and pop music to science and technology, and including literature, economy, health matters and other miscellaneous subjects. One of our most popular programmes is called 'Letterbox', in which, as the name suggests, the opinions of the listeners are aired. We encourage people to write to us not only about our programmes, but also about political developments, social problems, or any other subject that appeals to them. We received nearly 35,000 letters in 1991, and many of them were very thoughtful and provocative.

To whom do we broadcast?

We broadcast to everyone who wants to listen, and we know from the letters which we receive, and also from anecdotal evidence, that our listeners range from members of the Politburo to quite young schoolchildren. Because it is impossible for us to do audience research in China, until recently we had assumed that the majority of our listeners fitted the common World Service listener profile: young, male and educated. Although it is probably true that the majority are male, they cover an extraordinarily broad sweep of society, including armed police, entrepreneurs, Buddhist priests and peasants. A peasant recently wrote to say that, in a remote rural area where there was no television or newspapers, we were his only link with the outside world.

Future prospects

It is difficult to predict exactly how broadcasting will change in the future. We are assuming that in China, at least in the foreseeable future, short-wave radio will still be the most important means by which people will receive information from abroad about what is happening both in China and in the rest of the world. Even as China becomes more relaxed politically, as it no doubt will in time, it is still unlikely to have the same degree of media freedom as that in a pluralistic society. Looking five or ten years ahead, technology may have reached a point at which television satellite receivers are so small and so cheap that no government is able to prevent its people from owning them, and then our current listeners in China may be viewing World Service Television in Chinese, as well as listening to it in Chinese. We may have become bi-media! However, no matter what the medium, the aim will still be the same: to inform and to entertain.

APPENDICES

Appendix One:
A day in the life of
the Duiwaibu

ROBIN PORTER

This account is based on a composite of several days in the writer's experience at the Duiwaibu in 1979.

A typical day begins at 6 a.m. with the arrival at the office of the Duiwaibu's morning work-team for that day. On this particular day, several important stories are expected in the early morning news, so one of the Duiwaibu's senior cadres is heading the team, which is otherwise made up of two of the most promising younger journalists. All three are fluent in English, and will write their stories directly in English. At a meeting of senior cadres the previous evening it had been decided that Xinhua, responding to the current concern of the party, and following the lead given by the domestic press, should issue a piece to explain and promote the policy of economic readjustment. It was also expected that Deng Xiaoping would make an important speech that evening, which would be picked up by the morning press.

In the event, Deng's speech, a further exposition of the need to seek truth from facts, is carried in full in *People's Daily*. The team leader takes the translation of this speech as his first priority, while his two assistants settle down to other tasks. One deals with a report, obtained by telephone from the Foreign Ministry, of a meeting the previous day between Deng and a visiting American trade delegation, which he writes up in a form suitable for external release. The other, on the instructions of the team leader, writes up a digest of readers' letters published in *People's Daily* that morning criticizing privilege among party cadres, another matter over which the party is currently mounting a campaign. The work is interrupted by a telephone call from the Foreign Ministry to say that a prominent African leader has died, and that both the premier and Vice-Premier Deng have made expressions of condolence. One of the younger men puts aside the story he is working on to write up this urgent news.

By now it is 8 a.m., and the journalists on the regular daytime shift have begun to arrive, distributing themselves to their own sections elsewhere in the Duiwaibu. The head of the Economic Section is on this occasion to be 'editor for the day', with responsibility for directing and approving all the daytime work except for that produced by the morning work-team. He is an experienced journalist, although not quite so senior as the morning's work-team leader. Although he too attended the meeting to plan the work the previous evening and knows roughly what the work-team is likely to be doing, he none the less confers with the team leader to make sure that the same material is not dealt with twice over. He then tours the sections to see what each one is working on, returning after half an hour to check the first stories submitted to him – usually items begun the previous day.

For routine stories, it is at this stage that the principal editorial check is conducted by the editor for the day, although any journalist's story will normally have been seen by his section head before being handed to the editor, and along with all other stories will subsequently be quickly vetted by the head of the Duiwaibu or another very senior journalist before it goes out on the wire. The editor is concerned that the story should be accurate and complete in journalistic terms, that any translation from domestic news sources should be correctly done, and that the political line of the story should reflect the party's will on the matter being reported.

The first two stories to reach the editor's desk on this particular morning are both from the Economic Section and present few problems. In each case the task of the journalist has largely been to translate a story for which the research has been done elsewhere. One story is about the opening of a new gas pipeline across the upper reaches of the Yangtze, and has been sent in to the Economic Section by telephone from a Xinhua branch in Sichuan. The journalist who took the call knew what questions to ask to clarify the material; the story is complete and reasonably well written, and the editor passes it. The other story, also from a branch office in Sichuan, was sent in to Head Office by post, and has already been in the section for several days. It is about the development of animal husbandry in Sichuan. Although the theme is of ongoing concern, there is no particular piece of news on which to peg the story. But it is quite well written and of interest to the party at this time, so the editor lets it through. Usually some further amplification might be considered desirable for a story from a remoter branch, but in this case the delay and expense which would be incurred in obtaining it cannot be justified.

Meanwhile, in the morning work-team, the initial stories of the day have now been completed, been checked by the team leader, and been sent for final approval before being dispatched on the wire as a matter of urgency. The team leader has decided that a *Worker's Daily* editorial on the policy of economic readjustment would be a suitable vehicle for explaining the party's intentions in this area to readers outside China, and so has set to work translating it. His story, in English, will be a straightforward rendering of the editorial, attributed to *Worker's Daily*, and without further comment. His assistants are working on a story about the application of the new criminal law, which has been planned for several days, but which it has been decided will go out today. In several domestic newspapers this morning there are articles about trial proceedings, and so this seems the appropriate time to take the matter up. Using material from the newspapers and the notes that one of the journalists took several days previously in an interview with a professor of law at the Academy of Social Sciences, the two journalists put together a survey of how the law is being applied in different parts of China.

At this stage the editor for the day receives a story from the Political Section, and a discussion ensues. This piece is also about the new criminal law, but is a report of comments made by a vice-premier about the applicability of Chinese law to foreign nationals in China, and in certain circumstances to people deemed to have committed offenses outside China's borders. The point has been made by the foreign sub-editor that, as the interpretation stands, China appears to be claiming extraterritorial jurisdiction in certain circumstances outside its own borders.

Although it would be useful to put the piece out in conjunction with the other story on criminal law, and a vice-premier's remarks would usually be treated with urgency, it is felt that considerable damage might result if the story were to misrepresent either the remarks made or China's true position on this question. The decision is taken, after a brief consultation by telephone with the head of the Duiwaibu, both to re-check the story with the vice-premier concerned, and to consult the professor of law who had given advice on the other legal story. This piece was then put in abeyance, and would in the event re-emerge after clarification to appear in the *Xinhua Bulletin* three days later.

It is now 11 a.m. The morning work-team has completed its urgent work for the day. Its two junior members read the papers to keep abreast of other news, and occasionally take notes on items expected to form the subject of major developments later in the week. At around 2 p.m. they go down to the canteen, have a quick lunch and then go home for the day. The team leader is not so fortunate. He has been making notes for a meeting he must attend at 3 p.m. that afternoon, and which may well go on until 6 or 7 p.m. At this meeting of senior cadres from the various divisions and departments of Xinhua a broad plan of work will be laid out for the next month to six weeks. Since the National People's Congress will be meeting, and there will also be a week-long visit by a prominent Western leader, it will be a very busy time.

By now, stories from the regular sections are coming in one after another, and the editor for the day has a pile of them on his desk. One is a brief piece on the founding of a biochemistry society in Hangzhou, which a journalist in the Economic Section has taken from a Hangzhou newspaper, edited, and translated. Another, based on a report sent in by post from a Xinhua branch, describes developments in Korla, a town in the Gobi desert. Both stories are checked and approved. A third story, about a town somewhere in Hunan, is rejected because in the editor's view it is poorly written and contains little that could really qualify as news. The editor asks the journalist concerned to send a memorandum to the branch that submitted the story, explaining what Head Office would like to see in this type of report. By contrast, a story reporting China's two millionth operation using acupuncture anaesthesia, and describing the history of this use of acupuncture, has been exceptionally well put together; the earnest young journalist in the Cultural Section who wrote the story had researched it with great care, and, rather than rely on second-hand reports of the process, had gone himself to several major hospitals in the Beijing area to discuss the technique with the surgeons involved. His work is rewarded, and the story is passed without change. By 4 p.m. there is a lull in the proceedings. Most journalists are now working on material for submission on another day, or are scanning the papers for something else to write about. The editor has slipped away for an hour to attend the meeting to plan the coming month's work. Suddenly there is a telephone call that briefly throws the office into a panic. A foreign correspondent has discovered the Duiwaibu's telephone number, and against all the odds has succeeded in having himself put through with an inquiry about a story put out in the previous day's *Bulletin*. No one knows quite what to do. The editor is hurriedly sent for, while the caller waits on the line. The editor answers the caller's query, but politely points out that there is at present no established procedure to permit the Duiwaibu to respond directly to correspondents' inquiries. The Duiwaibu is thinking of experimenting with press conferences, but no decision has been taken.

Three more stories appear in the editor's basket at 5 p.m., towards the end of the normal working day. One is by an elderly woman journalist in the Cultural Section who studied at Columbia University before 1949. Ostensibly about the opening of the Dunhuang caves to tourism, the story gives a brief but comprehensive history of the famous paintings there, and places them in their social context. The story is based on a Luxingshe publicity release about the caves, much augmented from other sources and from the personal knowledge of the journalist involved. Another story is by a journalist in the Economic Section, and is based on a lengthy article in the *Shanghai Liberation Daily* about innovations in the Shanghai motor industry.

Both these stories are passed without alteration, but the third story, the final submission of the daytime shift, proves to be wholly unacceptable. It has been researched locally in Beijing by a staff member recently transferred from a branch in the interior, and is about experiments with a new type of solar panel. Unfortunately, the journalist has apparently not understood the principle of operation of solar heating panels, and this is quite evident from the text. The editor calls in the journalist responsible, and asks him to go back to the factory to research the story further. The editor substitutes an article from a file of spare copy in the Economic Section, a piece about the planting of new trees, vowing as he does so not to allow another tree story through until at least next week.

At 5.30 p.m. most of the Duiwaibu's day shift in the individual sections go home, and the night shift, or more accurately the evening work-team, comes on duty. Three out of four journalists working under a night editor are the core of this team, although they are assisted this evening by three journalists from the day shift who have stayed on to attend and report on two receptions and a performance by the visiting Royal Shakespeare Company.

In the early evening there is little for the night shift to do except to work on a report that has come in on the wire from a Xinhua branch in Shandong about a visit by an African military delegation to the East China Sea Fleet of the Chinese navy. Two journalists take the opportunity to go off to the room where the television is kept, to watch the news and to catch part of the football game between Beijing and a visiting Japanese team. Shortly after 9.30 p.m., the two journalists covering the banquets given for visiting delegations return to the office and begin to write up their 'protocol' stories in the particularly formal style reserved for reports of these functions. The journalist attending the Royal Shakespeare Company's performance also makes her appearance, and sits down to wrestle with the problem of writing a review that must also dwell on the value of the group's visit in reinforcing Sino-British friendship. In another office, a journalist has been in private conversation with the Ministry of Defence about an armed clash that occurred some two hours earlier on the border with Vietnam. He sits down to write an urgent piece about the incident, which, after approval by the night editor, he takes immediately up to the office where finished stories are sent out on the wire.

This evening business is slack, and all the work has been completed by 11.30 p.m. The night editor has checked each story carefully, but much of the news on the evening shift concerns questions of protocol and is written to a formula, so there is little in practical terms for him to do. He has been going over notes, given to him by a colleague, of the decisions of the afternoon meeting with regard to the plan of work for the coming month. He will have responsibility for leading a team that will report on the National People's Congress, and will have to choose the journalists who are to assist him, briefing them in advance on the resolutions that are likely to come up.

By half past midnight the work-team has dispersed and gone home. The day's work, as it has been sent out on the wire and will appear in the *Xinhua Bulletin* the following morning, comprises these stories:

Vice-Premier Deng Xiaoping urges people to seek truth from facts.
Workers' Daily editorial on economic readjustment policy.
China's premier expresses condolences on death of African leader.
Vice-Premier Deng mourns the passing of Third World leader.
American trade delegation signs agreement with China.
People's Daily publishes letters criticizing privilege.
New criminal law applied throughout China.
Sichuan lays gas pipeline across Yangtze.
Development of animal husbandry in Sichuan.
China biochemistry society founded in Hangzhou.
Developments in Korla – a town in the Gobi desert.
China has performed two million operations under acupuncture
    anaesthesia.
Dunhuang caves open to tourism.
Shanghai motor industry taps potential.
Three thousand new trees planted in Beijing.
Beijing banquet for visiting US trade delegation.
Somali military delegation visits East China Sea Fleet.
Academic exchange announced at banquet for Japanese guests.
English theatre troupe performs in Beijing.
Soldiers of the People's Liberation Army resist new Vietnamese
    incursion attempt.

Appendix Two:
The pattern of China's
external news

ROBIN PORTER

The output of the Duiwaibu in May 1979

It must be clear to any regular reader of the *Xinhua Bulletin* that there is a substantial degree of repetition in the news output of the Duiwaibu from day to day. Because of this, it is possible to classify news stories as belonging to one or other type and sub-type according to the subject matter, and to determine over time the relative importance attached by the party to the release of different types of 'news'. In the brief categorization offered below, delineation of an item as primarily 'political', 'economic', 'cultural', etc., reflects my experience of the distribution of stories among the various sections of the Duiwaibu. Further classification is based on a careful reading of the content of each story, and a decision as to what in essence it is about. This determination should not be taken in any way as absolute, but will give some idea of the pattern of news output. May 1979 has been chosen as a typical month in which the news was not distorted by the intrusion of a National People's Congress or party conference, and before there had been any significant impact on Chinese journalists of training in Western journalistic techniques.

The *Xinhua Bulletin* of May 1979 contained 1,848 news items.* Of these, 1,200 items, or nearly two-thirds, came from the Guojibu, Xinhua's International Division. These items originated overseas, and were about international events. The remaining 648 items were put out by the

---

*For the purpose of this paper, May 1979 is taken as having 30 days, since the *Bulletin* for 2 May was unobtainable at the time of writing.

Duiwaibu in Beijing, and were about developments in China. Of these stories, only 90 were principally political in content, while 120 dealt with economic developments and 67 covered cultural affairs in the broad Xinhua meaning of that term. A further seventeen stories dealt with health and medicine, and sixteen with sporting events. The other 338 news items all had to do with what were called at Xinhua 'protocol' stories, and recorded the comings and goings of delegations of many kinds from various countries.

Put another way, the Duiwaibu put out over the wire an average of twenty one news items per day. Eleven covered diplomatic and protocol matters, while the remaining ten stories recorded all the other news from China. Of these ten, on average three were political, four economic, two cultural, and one-half each day dealt with medicine and with sporting events. Within this breakdown, it is also possible to find a pattern of repetition of certain themes and types of story which will throw further light on Xinhua's objectives in its preparation of news for external consumption.

Political stories

In May 1979, the most significant political stories were those concerned with what might be called 'current campaigns' – that is, matters which were of particular ideological concern to the party at the time. Thus nine stories dealt with the theme of criticism, with the emancipation of thought, and with the need to 'seek truth from facts';[1] three dealt with party privilege;[2] two with the need for discipline among cadres and in society as a whole;[3] four with the question of democracy;[4] and three with the effects of rule by the Gang of Four.[5]

The past could be and was frequently invoked in support of current objectives: no fewer than thirteen stories were put out to commemorate the sixtieth anniversary of the May Fourth Movement of 1919,[6] while two others recalled the revolutionary careers of Li Dazhao and Xu Deheng.[7] Another story took note of a *Workers' Daily* article with a picture spread on Marx and Engels,[8] while four others cited model citizens from the population as a whole, three of them from the armed forces.[9]

Some stories were intended to appeal to specific segments of the

Chinese population, even though they formed part of the news for external consumption. Among these were two directed at the People's Liberation Army (PLA),[10] and another, a report of a speech by Kang Keqing, was aimed at young women.[11] As many as twenty items were dedicated to the nation's youth.[12] Other stories were directed towards a specific audience outside China: there were three Taiwan stories in May, urging contacts or in one case recording a defection by a Taiwanese to China;[13] and there were fifteen stories of the progress that it was claimed had been made by China's national minorities. Almost half of these were about Tibet or Tibetans.[14]

Some political stories were more simply a record of political developments or events presented in a straightforward reporting style. Of these, two related to preparations for People's Congresses at the national and Beijing municipal levels, two covered the third session of the Standing Committee of the Chinese People's Political and Consultative Conference, three recorded recent developments in the legal sphere, and another dealt with the role of trade unions in promoting production.[15]

Economic stories

Among the economic stories given greatest prominence, and placed towards the front of the *Xinhua Bulletin,* were those in which theoretical questions relating to the economy were discussed. Many economic stories had some theoretical point of reference, but, in May 1979, ten items dealt explicitly with theoretical issues in economic policy. Of these, for example, one came from a *Workers' Daily* article which discussed the relationship between moral and material incentives,[16] another was a call for democracy in planning on the communes,[17] while a third had its origins in a *People's Daily* article which discussed the role foreign technology should have in China's modernization.[18] Six of these ten stories were taken from other organs of the Chinese press.[19]

The great majority of economic stories reported on developments in agriculture (twenty nine) or in the manufacturing industry (seventeen). Some were of a general nature,[20] but most reported specific instances of progress. The latter tended to fall into one of two categories: some reported on the level of production and quality of output (production was invariably up, and quality improved),[21] and others focused on some specific innovation or a decision to diversify production, highlighting the ingenuity brought to the solution of a particular problem, frequently referred to at the time as 'tapping potential'.[22]

Another twenty two stories were concerned with development of the country's infrastructure. Of these, five were on the subject of mining or mineral resources, six on the generation of energy, six on transport and five on the construction industry.[23] A further nineteen items dealt with matters connected with the environment, including forestation, ornamental flowers and trees, water conservancy and irrigation, the conservation of animal and plant life, soil conservation, palaeotology, and pollution.[24]

Of the remaining economic stories, seven dealt with aspect of scientific and technical innovation,[25] six with tourism,[26] and three with population growth and birth control.[27] Two stories concerned joint ventures and foreign investment.[28] The remaining four stories dealt with the rate of domestic savings in South China, the provision of welfare facilities, and the economic effects of devastation from a tornado.[29]

Cultural stories

In 1979 the Cultural Section was still regarded as the poor relation of the Duiwaibu, a fact unfortunately reflected in its long-suffering staff, who were mostly women and trainee young men. The greatest number of the Cultural Section's stories, some twenty three items, concerned literary events and publications. Some of these registered the recent publication of translations of foreign literary or scientific work in Chinese; others recorded Chinese works rendered into English or other foreign languages.[30] Several stories marked the founding of new journals, and most of the remainder recorded the publication in Chinese of works covering the whole range of intellectual activity.[31]

Nine other stories dealt with the performing arts in China, including musical events, puppet shows, dance, acrobats, opera and the revival of Cao Yu's play *Thunderstorm*.[32] Six stories were about the fine arts, another six on archaeological finds and historical relics, and three more on the cinema and the inauguration of a new television channel in

Beijing.[33] Ten items were relatively short pieces on a range of commemorative items or events, such as the issue of special stamps on May Day, or the projected issue of gold coins on National Day.[34]

Six stories reported on developments in education, a subject that was generally left to journalists in the Cultural Section unless a major policy speech warranted treatment by the daily work-team.[35] Another item reported on a national conference on philosophy.[36] Finally, two stories of a theoretical nature were taken from *People's Daily*, one calling on people to 'create more art', and the other noting that a 'special commentator' (a senior official) had urged that a 'hundred flowers' should bloom once more.[37]

Health and medicine

In May of 1979, seventeen stories were put out about health and medicine, ranging from the health of newborn quadruplets to advanced medical research.[38] These items were also the responsibility of the Cultural Section.

Sporting events

The sixteen stories on sporting events taking place in China were the responsibility of no particular section, but rather were the work of two journalists with an interest in sporting activity.

The remaining 338 diplomatic and protocol stories were generally short pieces covering visiting delegations of all kinds, the signing of protocols, and diplomatic agreements.

Notes

1 (051204) 'Criticism must be welcomed, says *People's Daily*'; (050505) 'China must take its own road, says *People's Daily* editorial'; (051123) '*People's Daily* features article by *Guangming Daily* guest commentator', etc.

2 (051705) '*People's Daily* stresses importance of opposing special privileges', etc.

3 (052706) '*People's Daily*: Everybody must work hard', etc.

142

4 (050625) 'China will continue to expand democracy, says Shanghai newspaper', etc.

5 (050901) *'Liberation Army Daily* stresses education in treating followers of the Gang of Four'; (051046) 'Memorial meeting for famed actress Shu Xiuwen', etc.

6 (050356) 'Beijing meeting commemorated May Fourth Movement anniversary', etc.

7 (050311) *'People's Daily* article commemorated Li Dazhao', etc.

8 (050506) *'Workers' Daily* features pictures on Marx and Engels'.

9 (052703) 'Learn from combat heroes says *Beijing Daily* editorial'; (050602) 'Shanghai young workers devoted to socialist modernization', etc.

10 (051915) 'PLA cadres study economic questions', etc.

11 (051144) 'Kang Keqing discusses love, marriage and the family'.

12 (050332) 'Fifth Committee of All-China Youth Federation opens session'; (051310) 'Beijing young workers in campaign for socialist modernization'; (052217) 'China Youth says: Give guidance rather than find fault', etc.

13 (050612) 'Mainland meteorologists urge contacts with Taiwan colleagues'; (052112) 'Former Kuomintang airmen join Communist Party of China', etc.

14 (050421) 'Minority Representatives and Democratic Personages in Qinghai inspect rural areas'; (043013) 'Panchen's father elected additional member of CPPCC Tibetan Standing Committee'; (050606) 'College graduates volunteer to work in Tibet', etc.

15 (051513) 'Peng Zhen, Bo Yibo elected deputies to the Fifth National People's Congress'; (050424) 'CPPCC Standing Committee holds third session in Beijing'; (050819) 'China trains more cadres in politics and law'; (052301) 'Trade unions to lead workers in "Increase production and practice economy" drive', etc.

16 (050416) *'Workers' Daily* discusses relationship between mental and material encouragement'.

17 (050501) 'People's commune in Zhejiang province makes plans for production and distribution'.

18 (050807) *'People's Daily* calls for correct approach towards import of foreign technology and equipment'.

19 Two (050608 and 050807) were from the *People's Daily*; two (050416

and 050902) were from the *Workers' Daily*; one (051008) was from *China Youth News*; and one (050702) was from a newspaper in Liaoning.

20 (043018) 'Tianjin's industrial output up'; (051529) 'All-round development of Xinjiang's rural economy', etc.

21 (052111) 'Suzhou's silk industry flourishes'; (043008) 'Jilin province announces record agricultural growth'; (052612) 'China's southern provinces report good rapeseed harvests', etc.

22 (050203) 'New system for heating, drying introduced in Hangzhou'; (043011) 'Technical transformation boosts iron and steel production'; (052308) 'Seeds treated with electric current give higher yield', etc.

23 (051716) 'Large-scale capital in China's biggest coal field; (051528) 'Chinese power industry taps potential'; (050309) 'China's cement plants report successes in socialist emulation drive', etc.

24 (052108) 'Pollution control in Beijing'; (050403) 'Spring afforestation in Beijing'; (051804) 'Cherry blossom time in Qingdao'; (052324) 'Sichuan and Hubei store water against drought'; (052810) 'Chemical mulch used in China's agriculture and forestry'; (051710) 'Conservation areas for wildlife in China'; (051627) 'Veteran palaeontologist discusses bio-environmental control hypothesis', etc.

25 (050509) 'Major scientific achievements recognized', etc.

26 (050929) 'Shanghai starts pleasure-boat cruising', etc.

27 (051903) 'Successful control of population growth in Rudong County, East China', etc.

28 (051908) 'Chinese civil engineering company accepts foreign contracts', etc.

29 (052310) 'Bank savings rise in South China autonomous region'; (051228) 'Seven counties in Zhejiang province hit by tornado', etc.

30 (051702) 'Contemporary American short stories published in Shanghai'; (050820) 'English translation of *Dream of Red Mansions* now complete', etc.

31 (052214) 'Quarterly journal *Problems in the Philosophy of Science* to be published in Chinese'; (052220) 'Story of Naiserden Atainde re-published'; (052615) 'Collection of Qin Music to be published in twenty four volumes'; (050729) 'First issue of *General Knowledge* comes off the press', etc.

32 (051326) 'Spring concerts at West Lake'; (051650) 'Quanzhou puppetry revived'; (051249) 'New dance using classical style on Chinese stage';

(050921) 'The Chinese Wuhan Acrobats'; (051249) 'Chinese singers learn about Japanese opera', 'Cao Yu's *Thunderstorm* staged again', etc.

33 (052319) 'Naxi paintings on show'; (051319) 'Bronze chime bells unearthed'; (052120) 'Three-hundred-and-fifty-year-old map of the stars found in Fujian province; (051812) 'Life story of folk musician filmed'; (051309) 'New television station to start in Beijing', etc.

34 (043007) 'China issues May Day stamp'; (051613) 'China to issue gold coins in commemoration of National Day'; (051418) 'Zhou Enlai's letters presented to Chinese History Museum', etc.

35 (050704) 'Spare-time education for Beijing workers', etc.

36 (043009) 'National conference on philosophical research'.

37 (052109) '*People's Daily* articles on creating more art'; and (052906) 'Carry out Hundred Flowers in art, says *People's Daily* commentator'.

38 (052707) 'Largest ever acupuncture forum opens June 1st'; (052117) 'New methods to detect liver cancer in early stages', etc.